Stressed Out!

A woman's guide to stress management for hormone healing and weight loss success.

EMMA LOUISE KIRKHAM

Copyright © 2023 by Emma Louise Kirkham

All rights reserved. No part of this publication may be reproduced, distributed, or transmitted in any form or by any means, including photocopying, recording, or other electronical or mechanical methods, without the prior written permission of the publisher, except in the case of brief quotations embodied in reviews and certain other non-commercial uses permitted by copyright law.

First Edition
Published 30th June 2023

Disclaimer

All information contained within this book is for informational purposes only. It is not intended to diagnose, treat, cure or prevent health problems – nor is it intended to replace the advice of a qualified medical practitioner. Always consult your physician or qualified health professional on any matters regarding your health or on any opinions expressed in this program.

The information provided within this book is believed to be accurate based on the best judgment of the author, but the reader is responsible for consulting with his or her own health professional on any matters raised within. We do not assume liability for the information contained within this program, be it direct, indirect, consequential, special, exemplary, or other damages.

It is always advisable to consult your physician before changing your diet, starting an exercise program, or taking supplements of any kind, especially if you have pre-existing medical conditions. Also, in relation to any suspected conditions you may be seeking to address, you should always consult a doctor for any relevant testing requirements to either confirm or rule out your suspicions.

This book is dedicated to my amazing daughter, Shannon. My best friend, my parent at times, and the reason I strive for all that I do. I'm hoping that one day she will forgive me for passing my stressy-cow gene to her!

Stressed Out!

A woman's guide to stress management for hormone healing and weight loss success.

EMMA LOUISE KIRKHAM

Table of Contents

Introduction 11

Part 1: Introduction to Stress
How Does Stress Impact on Your Weight? 19
How Stressed Are You? 23
The Signs of Stress 25
What's Stressing You? 28
The Types of Stress 31
Work Related Stress 33
The Impact of Stress on Your Body 37
The Stress Pathways Explained 40
Positive vs Negative Stress 42
Long Term vs Short Term Stress 43
Stress and Anxiety 46
Social Anxiety 48
Stress, Anxiety, Pregnancy and Parenthood 58
PTSD 60
The Link Between Anger and Stress 62
Stress Resilience & Your Hormones 68
Your Ability to Cope 70
Avoiding Avoidance 77

Part 2: The Power of Mindset
What's Your Mindset? 87

It's all About Perception 90
Emotions and Feelings..93
Can You Regulate Your Emotions?....................................97
Your Thoughts Matter 101
Are You an Overthinker? 108
The Power of Positivity 118
Affirmations - Do They Really Work? 122
Compassion 128
Hope and Optimism..132
Gratitude 138

Part 3: Diet & Lifestyle
Manage Your Time to Manage Your Stress 143
Stress and Exercise 151
Stress and Gut Health 154
Stress, The Gut and Your Appetite....................................158
Stress and Your Eating Habits..160
Stress and Blood Sugar Balance...164
Don't Fear the Fat 168
Stress Busting Vitamins, Minerals and Herbs 172
Your Handy Stress Busting Shopping List......................182
Handy Stress Busting Meal Ideas......................................188
Breathing Techniques to Tackle Stress and Anxiety.....198

About the Author..205
Other Books by the Author...207
You May Also Be Interested In 209

Introduction

The first time we start to talk about stress, we tend to be in our teenage years. We complain about being so stressed to our parents only to be told, "You think you're stressed now, wait until you get older then you'll see what stress is!"

Sound familiar anyone? I know I got that line said to me more than once.

Yet, as we get older, we look back at our teenage life and begrudgingly admit that perhaps our parents were right after all as the endless cycle of life takes its burden on us.

We have the pressures of work, family life and housework to contend with. We see other women just smashing it and wonder why we can't have out sh*t together like they do.

We lay in bed at night, our mind racing with the thoughts of what we didn't manage to achieve that day or, what we need to get to done the following day. Hell, some of us are even planning the grocery list whilst having sex with our partners!

We simply don't switch off anymore and it's taking its toll on our minds and our bodies.

Stress is an increasingly common condition. In fact, it is said that 60-80% of doctors' appointments are stress related, and that 50% of absences from the workplace are because employees are stressed out.

There's also no definitive explanation as to what stress is although there are several definitions, each based on the individual researchers differing views and their different disciplines.

For example, when we look at the area of psychology and biology, stress is defined as the response of the mind and body to a demand placed upon it. In neuroendocrinology, it's a stimulus that results in the release of hormones and, in economics, it's when the resources a person values, such as a home or job, is threatened or lost.

What all of these definitions refer to is that we are under pressure. These pressures can come from various areas in our lives and can impact on each of us in differing ways. We will be looking at some of these throughout this book.

What I can also tell you, is that stress can play a huge role in your struggles to lose weight as it throws several of your other hormones out of balance.

Cortisol is a key player in the accumulation of abdominal fat, will send our blood sugars crazy, spur on food cravings and so much more. We will be looking at some of the ways this happens too.

The purpose of this book is to help you to understand and address these hormonal imbalances, tackle the stress and get you back on track when it comes to reaching your weight loss goals.

I've also designed this book to be more of an interactive journey. You'll be prompted throughout to take part in some exercises and I really hope you find these useful and beneficial.

In addition, I want you to know that even as a health coach, I have been guilty of living in a state of constant stress which had impacted on my mental and physical health, as well as heavily contributing to my hormone health and weight loss struggles.

From work related stress to relationship stress, I've had my fair share of mental health problems associated to it. The one big thing I remember from my darkest of days, was the feeling that the 'darkness' was taking me.

This darkness led to several suicide attempts, before one day something whispered to me 'What are you doing?'. Now, I'm not a very spiritual person but, that was like an enlightened awakening for me. No matter where that whisper came from, I'm so grateful for it because, if it was not for that whisper, I wouldn't be here today writing this book for you.

I do feel that I should add, if you are feeling at all suicidal or contemplating self-harm then you should go speak with a doctor. There is no shame in seeking help. In fact, it helped me massively when I was in my darkest of days.

I let my stress and anxiety take control of me but I came out of the other side, and I know you can too.

In this self-guided book, I'll be sharing with you the impact stress has on you, based on scientific research, along with steps you can take to regain control over it, rebalance those cortisol levels, and achieve greater success when it comes to healing your hormones from within. The same steps I followed myself to help improve my own wellbeing and improve my own health.

This book has been broken into three parts so you can easily keep dipping back into the parts you feel will benefit you the most.

Part 1 goes deep into the science to give you the lowdown on all things stress related, part two will look at tackling your mindset to help improve your ability to cope with stress and, part 3 will look at the dietary and lifestyle practices that can help alleviate the impact of stress.

However, if you find that a self-guided approach isn't working for you and you need more one-to-one support, drop me an email to **emma@emmalouisekirkham.com** to discussing working with me on a more personalized and deeper level.

But first, I want you to have a think about the reasons that you chose to buy this book. Why do you want to manage your stress levels? What do you hope to achieve from working through this book?

Writing your goals down can help keep them at the forefront of your mind which makes achieving them easier.

So, take a few moments to think about the questions below, and then make a note of them in the spaces provided below. You'll be able to refer back to these thoughts once you've completed the book and reflect on if it helped you achieve what you wanted it to.

Why do I want to tackle my stress levels? What impact is it having on my life and my health?

_____

_____

What goals do I hope to achieve from following the guidelines in this book? What changes do I want to see?

_____
_____
_____
_____
_____

I also want to give you a few tips for getting the most out of this book.

Keep an Open Mind

Before you go any further into this book ... be sure you are truly ready to make changes. You will be doing some soul searching, trying new techniques and implementing changes to both your lifestyle and your diet.

If you aren't ready yet, then you won't do this. You'll think it's the book that didn't work, but the reality is that you weren't ready for change. If that's the case, then don't stress ... it took me a few attempts to get there!

Make Sure You've Got Support

It's always easier to achieve your goals if you've got support around you. Don't be afraid to tell friends and family about what you are doing and why, that way it's going to be easier for you to make the changes and, you never know, they might even take part with you. The key to success is having a great support network around you.

Remember You are in Control

Yep, I said it. You ARE in control, despite what you might think. You hold the power in your own hands to heal yourself and regain control of your stress.

I can give you the tools and the advice, but it's down to you to implement it. Which goes back to what I said that you have to be ready to embrace change and to try out all the different techniques so you can discover which ones work best for you.

Share Your Successes and Your Journey with Me

I love to hear your success stories, and be your little cheerleader along the way, so show me what you're getting up to; whether you're trying out one of the techniques or getting creative in the kitchen, feel free to tag me on Instagram **@emmalouisekirkham** or by using the hashtag **#stressedoutbook**

So, if you really want to regain control over your stress and start seeing those positive changes both physically and mentally, grab yourself a cuppa (I'd recommend tea not coffee as coffee can disrupt your hormones and raise cortisol levels) and let's begin …

Part 1:
Introduction to Stress

How Does Stress Impact on Your Weight?

You probably noticed in the description of this book that I referenced how stress can hinder your weight loss attempts.

There's nothing more frustrating than thinking you are doing everything right yet not seeing the results on the scales (although photographs and measurements tend to be a more accurate way of gauging change as our bodies will naturally fluctuate by 4lbs each and every day).

I was in that same situation.

I was watching what I ate, cutting back on the alcohol (which was a huge part of my life, especially after moving to Portugal, and as I discovered along my own journey, was one of my default coping mechanisms to stress) yet, I still felt like I could give Shamu (you know, the Killer Whale at SeaWorld, in case you didn't get the reference) a run for her money in a bikini competition.

What was predominant in my life though was a hell of a lot of stress, combined with a side dose of being perimenopausal, and that stress was truly making all my other hormonal imbalances worse.

You see when you're already overweight, you're more than likely suffering from a toxic overload (*you can tackle that with my 28 Day Hormone Reboot Detox, check it out on my website*), estrogen dominance and blood sugar dysregulation. When you add stress into the mix, it's like throwing a fox into the chicken coop … sh*t is about to get crazy.

Stress is primarily linked to the hormone cortisol. Interestingly, when we think of stress, we always think of cortisol as being the primary hormone that is released however the release of this isn't immediate as it occurs after the release of epinephrine and norepinephrine (two other hormones we will be talking about later). This means that actually, cortisol takes longer to have an effect on the body but does tend to stick around longer than its counterparts.

We tend to have naturally fluctuating levels of cortisol throughout the day (when we aren't in overload that is). It's typically higher in the morning to help get us up and going for the day, being at its peak around 30 minutes after we wake up, and tapers off throughout the day to help us sleep at night when levels are at their lowest.

However, if you are a night shift worker, you will have differing fluctuations in cortisol levels. This is because your body will attempt to re-synchronize this to consider your work and sleep routine, as your body clock doesn't follow the typical morning/night cycle the rest of us do.

And, because you're a woman reading this (*apologies if you're not*) then your cortisol levels will also fluctuate with the hormonal changes that occur during your menstrual cycles. Oh, isn't being a woman trying to tackle stress such fun!

When cortisol is at optimal levels, which means our stress is under control and we live a Zen life, it plays a role in reducing inflammation in the body, regulates our emotions and helps to release the energy stored in our fat cells. Energy that we do not want to keep stored up if we are looking to address our weight!

However, when we have higher levels of cortisol being released, such as in times of chronic stress, the opposite occurs. We end up with more circulating glucose (blood sugars) and actually store the energy in our fat cells.

This results in issues such as being tired yet unable to sleep, as we can experience high cortisol at night instead of in the morning, as well as an increased craving for unhealthy and sugar-laden foods.

Elevated levels of cortisol will also increase anxiety, elevate blood sugar levels (as I just mentioned), cause fertility issues and oh, that one us women hate … increased fat around our abdomen. I guess I can't really get away with calling it a mummy tummy anymore considering the mini me is in her late 20's.

Not only that, but high cortisol levels are a cause of high estrogen levels (and can also cause low estrogen levels) and excess androgens, those male hormones that we do need a small amount of as women. This is why stress can also be linked to issues such as premenstrual syndrome and PCOS.

This then triggers what I like to refer to as the hormonal vicious cycle:

High Stress > High Blood Sugars > Sugar Cravings > Bacterial Imbalances in the Gut > Inflammation in the Body > Weight Gain > Further Stress on the Body.

And it keeps going just like that. Do you see how this can truly jeopardize your weight loss efforts?

But worry not, we're going to get that stress under control and by doing that you'll also start to regain control of those hormones and start seeing success with your weight loss efforts.

How Stressed Are You?

So, just how stressed are you?

Our experience of stress is determined by our perception of the situation, the threat of it and our ability to be able to handle it (we will cover more about this later).

It relates to how overwhelming we may find certain situations; how unpredictable our lives may feel to us and, how uncontrollable a situation may feel.

Our levels of perceived stress will differ from person to person. One person's stressful scenario may not be stressful at all to another person. Some of us will thrive under pressure whilst others may crumble at the slightest hurdle.

The initial idea of perceived stress was developed from the work of Dr. Sheldon Cohen and his colleagues back in 1983 and really, this concept refers to the imbalance between all of life's challenges, demands and struggles and our ability to cope with them.

Below you'll find a series of questions based on how you've felt over the last month to help give you an understanding of your own perceived levels of stress.

In the past month I have often felt:

- ☐ Upset because of something unexpected that happened
- ☐ Unable to control important things in my life
- ☐ Nervous or Stressed

- ☐ Unable to handle personal problems
- ☐ Like things are not going my way
- ☐ Unable to cope with all the things I need to do
- ☐ Like I am falling behind with everything
- ☐ Angry because things are out of my control
- ☐ Like everything is building up and I can't get on top of it

If you've ticked five or more of these boxes then chances are you are suffering from moderate to high levels of perceived stress. The more boxes you've ticked, the higher the level of perceived stress.

When you experience higher levels of perceived stress you may also notice behavioral changes such as an increased tendency to smoke (*or vape and drink too much alcohol, as it was in my case*), low energy levels and disrupted sleep. Oh, isn't stress fun!

But, worry not as I'm here to help, and throughout this book I'll be covering ways to help lower those stress levels and feel more able to cope.

TIP! *After you've worked through the book and implemented some of the tips and techniques, revisit this chapter and see if your levels of perceived stress have lowered.*

The Signs of Stress

Would you say that you can tell if someone is stressed just by looking at them?

Not always!

When we experience stress, a number of changes occur in the body physically, emotionally, behaviorally and cognitively. We will be looking at these in more detail as we go through this part of the book.

However, no two people will experience the same signs of stress as we are all unique in the ways we respond to it. This is why it can be so hard to know when someone is stressed, as some of use may internalize our stress and not display signs that are visible on the outside.

Below is a list of the different signs of stress on the body. Which of these do you notice when you are feeling stressed? Do they fall mainly in one category or are they spread over a few of the categories?

It's a good idea to get familiar with the signs of stress that you experience, as when you notice them starting to appear you can take steps to address them before they develop into a complete meltdown.

Physical Signs

- Tight neck and shoulders
- Back pain
- Sleep difficulties
- Fatigue or tiredness
- Racing heartbeat or palpitations not

linked to physical exertion
- Shakiness or tremors
- Sweating
- Ringing in your ears
- Dizziness or fainting
- Sensation of choking
- Difficulty swallowing

- Stomach pains
- Indigestion
- Diarrhea or constipation
- Frequent and urgent need to urinate
- Loss of interest in sex
- Increased frequency of minor illness (such as colds)

Behavioural Signs

- Grinding your teeth
- Unable to complete tasks
- Overly critical attitude
- Cruel, overbearing or aggressive behavior
- Fidgeting and restlessness
- Alcohol abuse
- Emotional eating or overeating

- Clenching fists
- Changes to sleep patterns
- Starting smoking or smoking more than usual
- Withdrawing from others and social activities
- Crying spells
- Walking or talking faster than usual

Emotional Signs

- Irritability
- Edginess
- Anger and/or quick temper
- Boredom
- Nervousness
- Feeling anxious or panicky
- Feelings of despair
- Lack of meaning in life
- Unhappiness
- Loneliness
- Depression
- Feeling powerless to change the things that are 'wrong'
- Feelings of insecurity
- Emotional outbursts

Cognitive Signs

- Continual worry
- Excessive overthinking
- Poor concentration
- Difficulty in remembering things
- Unable to think clearly
- Indecisiveness
- Loss of sense of humor
- Lack of creativity
- Mental confusion

NOTE: *Many of the symptoms of stress are similar to serious health conditions such as heart disease, breathing disorders and thyroid problems. If you have any concerns about your symptoms always pay a visit to your doctor or a medical practitioner. Better to be safe than sorry!*

What's Stressing You?

During one of my bouts of stress, anxiety and depression, way back in 2011 (*oh yep, I was diagnosed with the job lot!*), one of my work colleagues turned to me and said: "You've got a good job, a home, a husband, and kids. What do you have to be stressed and depressed about?"

That one phrase shows the utter lack of understanding around mental health, and it's one of the most frustrating things someone experiencing this can hear.

We don't know WHY we feel like we do, especially when it's related to depression. We actually feel disconnected from ourselves, detached from our emotions.

Oh, how we wished we felt better … but we just can't get to grips with it because, we've reached that point where we've tipped over the edge of being able to identify when a potential stressor is on the horizon because EVERYTHING is a stressor.

Luckily, mental health is more widely acknowledged and spoken about these days. We have more explanations as to what causes it and why it happens, and by the end of this book you'll be fully armed with all this knowledge too.

The causes of stress are typically related to life events. These life events that challenge us are known as a stimulus and these stimuli can cause anxiety or stress. When they do they become known as a stressor.

You can never escape stress completely because there are always going to be major changes in your life that will have an impact on your stress levels and feelings of tension. Some of the main ones include:

- **Home and Family Life:** Such as bereavement, conflict with partners, children or other family members, divorce or relationship breakdown, pregnancy, or even, getting married.

- **Work and Finances:** Such as bankruptcy or serious debt, loss of your job or changing jobs, setting up a new business, trouble in the workplace, changes to your work schedule.

- **Health:** Such as accident or injury, miscarriage, abortion, diagnosis of a life-threatening illness, unknown and unexplained medical concerns, sudden changes to your appearance or weight or, sudden changes to your sleep patterns

- **Personal and Social Events:** such as moving house, becoming homeless, being bullied, the loss of a pet, loss or lack of social life, arguments with a friend, getting a new boss at work or getting new neighbors.

However, we will all respond differently to the different challenges that life throws at us, so as I said earlier, what may be stressful for one person may be nothing more than a minor challenge to another person.

Typically, the more negative experiences that occur for you, the more stress you may experience (depending on your thoughts and feelings around the said situation) which can then lead to a further decline in your mental or physical health. I'll be talking about these later.

The important thing to remember here though is, we can't change the events that happen around us, or to us, but we can change how deal with them and how we cope with them.

Being aware of what is stressing you and creating an action plan for addressing these stressors, as well as changing how you view the situation, can help you cope and adapt better, as well as helping to alleviate those stress levels a little.

Next time you face a life challenge, ask yourself the following questions:

- What feelings or emotions do you experience when you think about this event?

- Why do you feel this way? *Keep asking yourself 'why' for each answer you get until you get the root of the feeling or emotion as the first few answers won't be the deepest rooted one. I did say we'd be digging deep and soul searching!*

You can also consider what happened in the lead up to this challenge, and what occurred after it, to really explore your feelings and thoughts.

The Types of Stress

We just looked at the life experiences that can influence your levels of stress, but stress itself can be categorized further.

There are four common areas of stress which were identified by Karl Albrecht, Ph.D. back in 1979 and these are:

- **Time Stress:** we have too much to do and not enough time to do it in.

- **Encounter Stress:** we worry about social interaction at gatherings such as parties or conferences.

- **Situational Stress:** this is based on a specific event or situation such as being in a minor car bump, breaking up with a partner or the first day at a new job. It's generally a short-term acute type of stress that doesn't tend to last long.

- **Anticipatory Stress:** we worry about what's going to happen in the future which can relate to an event such as having to travel alone, or can be a perceived worry such as worrying about what someone will think of you.

In addition to this, stress can impact us in different ways. These are known as physiological stressors and/or psychological stressors, in other words, stress that effects either the body or the mind (or both).

Physiological stress can include:

- Chronic illnesses
- Physical pain
- Extreme temperature fluctuations
- Lack of sleep
- Recovery from an injury

Psychological stress can include:

- Needing to have difficult conversations with loved ones
- Preparing to give a talk or speech
- Threats to your self-esteem
- Bullying
- Maltreatment or cruelty
- Boredom

Work Related Stress

At the start of this book, I mentioned my own encounter with work related stress. It was back in around 2010/2011 when I worked at Barclays, back in the days where we were expected to sell everything to anyone. Hey, if we could sell Granny back to her children it was a win!

High pressure selling has never been my style, if I saw a true need then yes, I'd approach it but, I was never huge on trying to force loans and insurance policies on people for the sake of making a sale. So, the job took its toll on my mental health and my wellbeing.

My mood had started to diminish, I didn't seem to enjoy anything anymore and I dreaded the alarm going off each morning as I knew that meant I had to go into work.

I remember getting in my car one morning to drive to work. I made it to the bottom of the road but then had to pull over as my heart was racing, I felt dizzy and I felt like my chest was being squeezed. It was a panic attack. I'd never had one before, I was terrified ... what was happening to me?

I phoned work to say I couldn't go in as I was unwell, made an appointment for the doctor and then, had around 2 months off work diagnosed with work related stress and anxiety.

For some people, they thrive under pressure at work, for others (*like me, in that instance*) they crumble under the demands, too afraid to admit they have more on their plate than they can handle for fear of judgement or losing their job or, because what they are doing isn't aligned with their values. This is when burnout occurs.

It's actually estimated that around 1 million Americans miss work each day due to stress, and in the UK 822,000 people suffer from work-related stress. That's no small number, so trust me when I say, you're not alone if you do suffer from this.

In fact, as a woman aged between 35 - 44, you are 67% more likely to have work-related stress than your male work colleagues.

Some common workplace stressors include:

- No level of control or influence in organizational decision making

- Conflict with colleagues (internal and external to the company)

- Trying to juggle work alongside personal issues

- Trying to keep working when physically or mentally unwell

- Job environment and working conditions

- Not being given enough breaks

- Being given more workload than you can handle

The problem that occurs within workplaces, is that people don't always recognize that others are under stress (*remember how I said you can't always tell by looking that someone is stressed*).

This is not only down to the signs differing from person to person, but also, because we all have different perceptions and mindsets when it comes to stress. Some view it as a positive thing and some view it negatively.

So, if your boss has a mindset that stress is good because it's a challenge and a positive thing to embrace, they won't see that you have a very different view and are feeling the pressure. Alternatively, they could just be a bit of a knob and not give a damn because they are too focused on reaching sales targets!

Occupational burnout is a term used to describe when you become physically, mentally or emotionally exhausted by your job. When this occurs you my feel like you are overwhelmed with work tasks, you may struggle to cope when additional tasks are given to you, your work performance declines and, the stress no longer confines itself in the workplace but makes its way into your home life too.

In today's modern world, it's incredibly easy for work to make its way into our personal life, and therefore cause us further stress, thanks to technology. Gone are the days of work being solely 9 till 5. In fact, many of us feel the need to respond to work messages and emails outside of work hours, simply because they have pinged through on our mobile devices.

When you feel like technology is taking over your life and putting additional pressure on you, it's time to take some time out. Put the phones on 'do not disturb' outside of work hours ladies, for the sake of your stress, your hormones, and that holy grail of being at your ideal weight!

Because, when we experience those high levels of burnout, it impacts on our diet, making us choose foods that do not serve us well. In addition to this, we may have a lack of motivation to exercise, and our sleeping patterns are disrupted; three of the key areas that are linked to weight gain and obesity, and therefore, hormone imbalances.

INTERESTING FACT!

The word 'Karoshi' in the Chinese, Japanese and Korean languages actually means: "overwork death" or in simpler terms, death by overworking. At least they acknowledge the darker side of workplace stress and the excessive burdens often placed upon us, even if it is a little dark!

However, when it comes to the workplace, a demanding workload isn't the only thing we have to worry about. We may encounter conflict with our colleagues or even workplace bullying, which can have a huge impact on out mental wellbeing.

We may also find ourselves under pressure during company mergers or restructures, upcoming redundancies or any other issues that may have us worrying about losing our job and facing financial hardship.

When you are looking to tackle workplace stress, many of the techniques in this book will help you develop your stress management skills both in and out of work so that you can restore some balance into your life (and your hormones).

Over the course of this book, we will be looking at techniques such as mindfulness, being aware of your personal values and honoring them, learning to communicate effectively and honestly about your capabilities, as well as how physical activity and a healthy diet can also help.

The Impact of Stress on Your Body

We've looked at some of the causes of stress that occur in our lives, now let's take a look at the impact it has on your body .... Be warned, we're going deep into the science (because I'm a geek for the science)!

Stressors can cause a biological change in the body that spurs on the release of our stress hormones (such as that cortisol I mentioned earlier). These hormones are what cause the physical changes in our body such as that rapid heartbeat. This is known as the "stress response".

The stress response system begins with a stimulus, for example, a loud noise behind you when you are walking down the street at night. The brain then considers if this noise is a potential threat. This occurs in the amygdala, a part of our limbic system located in the brain.

Our limbic system is what modulates our endocrine system and the release of hormones, and our autonomic nervous system which controls our automatic bodily functions such as breathing, digestion and heartbeat. In addition to this is helps regulate our emotions, behavior, motivation levels and supports our long-term memory.

The limbic system includes our hypothalamus, which links our endocrine system to our nervous system, the amygdala which is responsible for fear conditioning, emotional arousal and our emotion driven memory, our hippocampus which is responsible for our learning, memory and processing of stimuli, our cingulate gyrus which link actions to emotional responses, our corpus callosum which connects the right and left brain hemispheres and our thalamus which controls our sensory and motor signaling, consciousness, sleep and alertness.

That's a lot that goes on in the brain right, but let me share this sneaky little bit of info with you … our brain can also become overloaded with toxins. Sleep is critically important for brain health as when we sleep our neural pathways widen to help remove toxic fluids from our brain.

Back to the stress response … So, if our amygdala detects a threat our hypothalamus goes into action, activating our autonomic nervous system. This stimulates the secretion of a hormone called corticotrophin also known as adrenocorticotropic hormone (ACTH), which is involved in our stress response and produces the hormone vasopressin, also known as antidiuretic hormone (ADH).

When it comes to stress and our hormones, balance is always key. With stress, the optimal state is to achieve balance in both our sympathetic nervous system (SNS) and our parasympathetic nervous system (PSNS).

The sympathetic nervous system is involved with our fight, flight or freeze response, whereas the parasympathetic nervous system is the one that regulates our rest and digest system.

If one is overactive, the other becomes limited in use or in simpler terms, if the SNS is overactive due to stress and that fight or flight response, the PSNS tends to shut down bodily functions such as digestion in order to preserve energy to escape the threat.

Let me give you an example of this …

Back in caveman days, when the caveman encountered a wild beast, their stress response system would kick in. They would need to make a rapid decision as to whether they would need to run and escape, or whether they would stay and fight (*that sabretooth tiger could fed the family for a week, after all*).

Whilst this decision making is taking place, those chemical changes in the body are occurring, stopping our non-vital functions such as digestion and reproduction and increasing our adrenaline levels to support us as we run away or stand and fight.

Freeze was a term coined afterwards, and it's the term used for when where we stop dead in our tracks, like a deer in the headlights that just freezes and stares at you before eventually running away.

Either way, the SNS and the PSNS are influenced in this scenario, with the SNS being overactive in that moment of danger which is why stress has so many knock-on effects in the body.

So, as you can see, our body can react differently depending on the stress it is facing. We also have different pathways in the body that may be intensified during this moment of life or death decision making.

For example, if the threat is immediate and requiring a fast response (such as our caveman example) we tend to go through the sympathetic-adrenal-medullary (SAM) axis.

If we have more time to think about the situation (*or overthink it, if you're like me*) we tend to activate our hypothalamic-pituitary-adrenal (HPA) axis.

We will look at both of these pathways next.

The Stress Pathways Explained

The Sympathetic-Adrenal-Medullary (SAM) Axis

The SAM axis is the stress pathway activated when we face an immediate threat or danger and must make a sudden decision or a rapid response.

When the SAM axis is activated the sympathetic nervous system releases acetylcholine which activates the adrenal medulla (a part of our adrenal gland) and causes the release of neurotransmitters, including epinephrine (adrenaline) and norepinephrine (noradrenaline), into the blood stream.

These neurotransmitters will re-route our blood flow to increase our heart rate and feed our brain and muscles in order to allow that rapid response to danger.

In addition to this, epinephrine and norepinephrine will increase blood sugar levels, blood pressure, metabolic rate and breathing rate. The changes they cause to our blood flow patterns will make us more alert, slow down our digestion and decrease the activity of our reproductive system.

In other words, unnecessary bodily functions are put on pause (as I've previously mentioned) until the threat has been dealt with. Once the 'danger' has passed, normality generally resumes and hormones levels balance themselves back out.

In the short-term, activation of the SAM axis isn't usually an issue but, when we experience long-term stress problems with our balance of hormones and our fertility can be impacted.

The Hypothalamic-Pituitary-Adrenal (HPA) Axis

The HPA axis is activated when we have a lot of time to dwell on a situation or worry about it. This can occur when we are afraid or anxious for prolonged periods of time.

When the HPA axis becomes activated, we experience an increase in the levels of corticotropin-releasing hormone (CRH) and vasopressin in our bloodstream.

Corticotropin-releasing hormone, which is secreted from the hypothalamus, triggers the release of adrenocorticotropic hormone (ACTH) from the pituitary gland.

This is then transported to the adrenal gland where it effectively instructs the adrenal gland to release more of those not-so-great stress hormones including cortisol, epinephrine and norepinephrine which can lead to a stress hormone overload.

Vasopressin induces the tightening of our blood vessels, causing our blood pressure to increase. When this happens, our body is working hard to try to pump our blood through these narrowed blood vessels, which is why we often notice an increase in heart rate when we are anxious or tense.

In addition to this, vasopressin also increases the reabsorption of water by our kidneys so our urine becomes more concentrated which can lead to kidney problems.

However, usually when the perceived stress (*we will be looking at perception in part 2*) has dissipated, vasopressin and corticotropin-releasing hormone levels start to go down and the neurons in the hippocampus start to calm down the HPA activity.

Positive vs Negative Stress

So far, we've concluded that stress is bad. However, stress can be a positive thing as it is what initiates our inbuilt survival mode (*think back to the caveman example from earlier*) which can help to keep us alive and, keep us challenged.

Eustress is the term used to describe the positive form of stress. This is the type of stress response that challenges and stimulates us. It's designed to motivate us and enhance our performance. Eustress is linked to emotions such as hope, satisfaction, commitment, flow and meaningfulness.

Think about it this way, if we didn't have a certain amount of pressure we would soon become bored. Things would be too easy, there would be no challenges, and we'd become dissatisfied and restless. Where would be the fun in life?

When it comes to these challenges and pressure, it's about how we respond to to them. Our responses influence if the stress levels become too much and, if we feel unable to cope we shift from eustress into distress.

Distress is the term used for negative stress, which does tend to rule the roost these days for many of us. It is the type of stress associated to all the negative feelings such as hopelessness, overwhelm and loss of interest. It can be demotivating and decrease performance in both your personal and professional life.

You'll notice as you work through this book that, in part 2, we delve into fostering a more positive mindset as a method for tackling stress and I really hope you find the activities and practices beneficial and enjoyable.

Long Terms vs Short Term Stress

We've looked at so many factors around stress already, have you realized there's far more to it than you may have thought at first?

I know it can seem a bit overwhelming, plus there's a lot more information that I want to share so that you understand all the ins and outs of stress (*science geek, remember!*)

You're about halfway through part one so, if your head is feeling fried, go and take a break. This isn't Netflix, there's no need to binge read, you can dip in and out as you need.

However, if you're feeling ready and you're raring to keep going, let me educate you further as we look at the duration of stress ...

When it comes to stress duration, there are two types of stress; short-term (acute) and long-term (chronic). We've touched on both of these already, but now I'm going to discuss them in more detail.

Which category of stress we experience will relate on our view of stress overall (i.e. positive vs negative) and our ability to cope with it (that section is yet to come).

Acute stress is generally the shortest time scale for stress. It's a brief yet intense feeling of stress that can last for minutes, hours or a few days. Acute stress typically lasts less than four weeks and can occur due to a car accident, nerves about an upcoming exam or interview, or an upcoming deadline for example.

Acute Stress Disorder is a type of stress that occurs after a traumatic event such as a death, natural disaster, etc. As I've already said, this typically lasts less than 4 weeks however, if it lasts longer than 4 weeks it becomes classified as chronic stress.

Chronic stress is a persistent type of stress. Stress is classified as chronic when it has been consistent for at least six to twelve months. It occurs when we face difficult situations or concerns, such as poor living or working conditions, relationship difficulties, financial struggles or ongoing health problems.

Another type of stress is episodic acute stress. This type of stress is intermittent and arises from short-term difficulties or concerns. It is a type of stress that repeats itself over a period of six months or more and can occur due to regular issues that arise such as periodical work projects or deadlines, monthly visits from the dreaded mother-in-law (*not that all mother-in-law's are bad*) or regular competitive sports.

Interestingly, when it comes to chronic stress the addition of further acute stress can either worsen or improve the situation. Let me share a couple of examples with you:

Karen suffers with chronic ill health. She doesn't work because of it, so her husband is the main breadwinner. However, Karen's husband … let's call him Bob … has just lost his job. So now, Karen and Bob are worrying about their finances. This added worry on top of her chronic health condition is making her stress levels much worse.

On the flip side, we've got Sally. Sally has been experiencing chronic stress for the last seven months due to work pressures and the difficulties she was experiencing in her failing marriage. When her husband decided to pack his bags and leave, she could have crumbled but instead, Sally felt a huge burden of relief and is now finding she can handle her work pressures much better and feeling much happier in herself.

So, just as with our view of stress, the addition of further stress can be either positive or negative depending on the situation and your perception of it.

DISCLAIMER: *I am not encouraging you all to go and leave your partners so you can handle work stress better. This was merely an easy way to explain my point. Divorce lawyers, I am not responsible for anything that occurs after my book has been read, no liability here!*

Stress and Anxiety

Now, we can't talk about stress without talking about anxiety as the two are often closely intertwined with each other however, they are not the same thing despite often being confused with one another.

Around one third of us are likely to experience some form of anxiety at some point in our life. It is generally a sense of worry, nervousness, unease or fear. It can occur when faced with an upcoming event like a job interview, a first date, or a work presentation.

For most of us it will pass quickly but for some, prolonged periods of anxiety can have an impact on our sense of wellbeing causing issues such as headache and being more susceptible to cold viruses.

Anxiety, just like stress, is normal. You're not a weirdo if you have bouts of anxiousness, but if that anxiety is continuous and long-lasting it can actually increase your stress levels further, which is why they are interlinked.

The symptoms of anxiety include:

- Increased heart rate
- Sweating
- Headaches or Migraines
- Dizziness
- Upset Stomach
- Needing to urinate more often than usual
- Difficulty breathing or shortness of breath
- Muscle tightness or twitching

- Shaking or trembling
- Difficulties sleeping
- Lack of libido
- Increased occurrence of minor illnesses (such as colds)
- Restlessness or fidgeting
- Nail biting
- Irritability
- Forgetfulness
- Feeling tense and/or jumpy
- Nervousness
- Poor Concentration
- Feelings of unease or dread

The symptoms of anxiety are also very similar to those of depression, which is why the two conditions are often confused with one another. However, many people are unfortunate enough to experience both, as was my case.

Anxiety is also categorized in two forms; state anxiety, which is a temporary state of anxiety and occurs from the uncertainty of a situation, and trait anxiety, which is longer lasting, more intense and frequent in occurrence and, it can also be genetic, as in it runs in the family *(I'm pretty sure my daughter is not thanking me for that genetic gift)*.

Learning to understand your thoughts and feelings can help tackle high levels of anxiety which is something we will be looking at in part 2 of this book.

Social Anxiety

Keeping on the theme of anxiety, another form of it that can have you wanting to embark on a 365-day hibernation is social anxiety.

If you find yourself getting anxious in social situations (*I know I do*) then rest assured you're not alone as it's estimated that 25-39% of the population experience it at some point during their life.

In fact, as a bit of an introvert I find it really hard to go on video of social media and, if you put me in a room full of strangers, I'm a nervous wreck, feel socially awkward, and prefer to hide away in a corner.

Social anxiety tends to refer to the feeling of fear or anxiety we experience in a social situation. These situations can include:

- Eating in a public place
- Making a phone call in public
- Meeting strangers
- Being observed at work
- Going to a party or social gathering (such as a wedding)
- Working in small groups
- Giving a talk to a large audience

You can see from the range of situations this can apply to why so many of us will have had some experience of social anxiety at one point or another. Alternatively, you might look at this list and think none of it applies to you, if that's the case fantastic, but remember that what might not be an issue for one person, could be a huge cause of anxiety for someone else.

I remember when I was at university as a mature student back in my late 20's, and every time I had to give a presentation in class I would feel sick, tremble and go into utter panic.

I'd stand and deliver my presentation whilst experiencing these feelings, giving a huge sigh of relief once I was done. The funny thing was, everyone said how confident I came across ... if only they had known my internal turmoil inside! Proof again, that how someone feels isn't always visible on the outside.

Another biggie for me is eating with someone you're on a date with, especially those first couple of dates. I worry so much about spilling food down myself or the date thinking I haven't eaten in a year (*as this girl has a good appetite!*).

The problem with high levels of social anxiety is that it really does mess your social life up. The reason for that is because you would much rather avoid a situation that makes you anxious than face it head on. When this happens, it's known as social avoidance.

Social avoidance refers to the extent to which you will avoid doing certain things because of your social anxiety. Do you outright avoid eating out in public? Turn down invitations to events because you are far too anxious about going?

When you are socially anxious, chances are you are worried or fearful about at least one of the following:

- Being judged
- Being the center of attention

- Being embarrassed or humiliated
- Accidentally offending someone

Now, the latter has never been the cause of my own social anxiety. I'm the queen of accidentally offending someone, either with my dark and slightly twisted humor, or my incapability to think before I speak. I'm the type of girl who says what she thinks without thinking about what she says.

Now being judged, that's a whole different kettle of fish although, it's kind of ironic that I write books and put them out there to be judged. Maybe the difference is down to my beliefs. I believe my books will help people address their areas of concern and help them lead better lives. I'll let you be the judge of that!

Social anxiety disorder steps it up another notch. It's the more severe and longer-lasting form of social anxiety, and it is incredibly common. In fact, it's the third most common mental health disorder with 7% of the population suffering from this at any one time.

You are also more likely to suffer from social anxiety disorder if you also suffer with another mental or physical illnesses ... fantastic news if your stress and anxiety is also combined with depression, not!

However, for most of us (approximately the 25 to 39% of the population who feel socially out of place at one point or another) the feelings are temporary and short lasting.

Here's an interesting fact for you thought ... the one thing you avoid (being social), can actually be one of the things that can help you. This is because social bonding with another person (or animal) has been found to help lower levels of loneliness, depression and anxiety?

Oh, and it's all down to our hormones too!

Namely, the hormones oxytocin and dopamine who communicate with the pre-frontal cortex in our brain and the nucleus accumbens (a collection of neurons in the brain that plays a role in our motivation, reward, pleasure and survival instincts) strengthening the connections between them.

This is also the same thing that occurs when we pair up with another human (you know, in a romantic way ... *wink, wink*). I guess that explains all the crazy cat ladies out there, or crazy dog lady in my case (*apologies to the cat lovers out there reading this*).

What you always need to remember is that these feelings of unease and social anxiety are there to protect us. By understanding them and applying some of the techniques we will be covering in this book, you'll be better equipped to handle social awkwardness (*as I like to call it*) with ease.

I've also got another technique you can try to help improve those feelings of social anxiety. That technique is known as mental rehearsal and we will be giving it a try in a moment.

Mental rehearsal can be really useful when preparing for things like job interviews, meeting someone new, having to have a difficult conversation with someone, and similar specific situations.

It's a cognitive technique that focuses on a positive internal state, words, images and senses which will help to provide a more favorable outcome. Or, in simpler terms, portraying an air of being cool, calm, collected and well-rehearsed when faced with a potentially stressful situation.

Now, mental rehearsal can consist of a series of methods, one of these is the best/worst/most likely scenario. You see, our brain seems to automatically default to negative and we think of the worst (especially if you're a pessimist, more on that in part 2), even though the chances of that worst outcome are slim. So, we need to look at the other possible outcomes and the likelihood of them happening.

Let's put this technique into practice.

ACTION TIME!

Think of an upcoming situation that is making you feel anxious, it may be a party you have been invited to, or a presentation you need to give. Think of the situation as an "If I …" statement and make a note of the situation below:

If I … (*e.g. go to the party on Saturday*)
_____
_____
_____

Okay, now thinking about if you do the situation above, what is the WORST thing that could happen?

_____
_____
_____
_____
_____
_____
_____

What are the chances of this happening (answer as a percentage)?

What is the best thing that could happen?

_____
_____
_____
_____
_____
_____
_____

What are the chances of this happening (answer as a percentage)?

What is most likely to happen in this situation?

_____
_____
_____
_____
_____
_____
_____

      Did you see from this exercise that your brain can drastically overthink a situation when in all likelihood, the chances of the worst-case scenario have a small chance of actually occurring?

      When I was younger, I always used to think the worst. In my mind, if the worst happened then I was expecting it. The same applied to people, I expected the worse from them as then I wasn't left disappointed by them.

In all honesty, that train of thinking was not in line with who I am, nor my values. Nowadays, I try to see the best potential in people and events. It's not always easy and yes, sometimes I'm still left disappointed, but it's a much nicer way to live.

Now, we will look at mentally rehearsing for the MOST LIKELY scenario …

When we are looking at a most-likely scenario, we need to first have an idea of what we want the end outcome to be and then we reverse engineer our plan from there. I guess it's similar to when we are in business, we have an end goal and must work backwards to plan out how we will get from where we are now to where we want to be.

Let's give it a try …

Thinking back to the most likely scenario from the previous exercise, what is the outcome you want to achieve from the situation?

_____
_____
_____
_____
_____
_____
_____
_____

When have you been in a similar situation before? What went well in that situation and how can you build upon that?

_____
_____
_____
_____
_____
_____

Who do you know who was in a similar situation and handled it incredibly well? What did they do to handle it so well? Was it something they said? How they portrayed themselves? Was it something they did? How can you apply these qualities to your own situation?

_____
_____
_____
_____
_____
_____

With all this information, what do you feel you need to do now in order to help reach your desired outcome (e.g. practice, research, etc)?

_____
_____
_____

What could be fun or positive about the situation? What could you gain from the situation (e.g. new skills, new friends, etc)?

What can you do to grow and develop personally or professionally from this situation?

Once you have an idea of how you want the situation to occur, practice it over and over again until you feel confident in your ability to portray yourself the way you want to.

Be sure to put this into practice every time you have a stressful situation coming up. The more you do it, the more in-tune with yourself and your feelings you will be, and the exercise and visualizations will also become much easier.

Oh, and here's my absolute favorite phrase, and one to live by ...

Fake it, until you make it!

When I first started training people in the body contouring treatments I was so nervous, especially as some of my clients were either also teachers in the beauty industry or medical professionals (doctors or nurses). I honestly felt so intimidated, so I had to take a deep breath and just do my thing.

In other words, I may not have felt confident in those situations, and my anxiety was truly through the roof, but I just faked my confidence ... and the feedback from the trainees was 5-star!

Stress, Anxiety, Pregnancy and Parenthood

Now, we are all women reading this (*or at least, you ladies are my target audience, no offence meant if you're a guy reading this book*) so, it's worth popping a short section in about stress, anxiety and its impact on fertility and pregnancy because, what is more stressful than parenthood?

I've already touched upon the fact that stress can impact on fertility and make it more difficult to conceive, which means if you're planning to bring a mini you into the world you also need to get on top of your stress.

Just as we spoke of the HPA axis previously and its role in stress, our fertility involves another pathway known as the HPG (hypothalamic-pituitary-gonadal) axis.

When this axis is activated it releases gonadotrophin-releasing hormone (GnRH) which supports the production of estrogen and testosterone and maintains a healthy reproductive system in both men and women.

The HPA axis and the HPG axis are linked (*go figure*) so, when the HPA axis is activated it puts us into that fight or flight mode, and systems deemed as unnecessary (such as reproduction) are shut down.

This applies to men just as much as women, so if the man in your life is always stressed it could also be impacting on the quality of his sperm too!

What if you're already pregnant? How can stress impact on you and your unborn child?

It's incredibly common for women to experience stress or anxiety during pregnancy, especially with a first child or if there have been problems with previous pregnancies. In fact, it's been estimated that 10-50% of women suffer from anxiety during pregnancy.

Despite cortisol levels naturally rising during pregnancy, as it plays a role in fetal development, too much maternal stress can impact on an unborn child's development. Maternal stress has been linked to an increased risk of premature birth and low birth weight. In addition to this, high stress in mum can result in high stress levels for baby.

Researchers carried out blood cortisol level tests (from a heel prick blood test) on babies and discovered that babies of highly stressed mums had increased levels of cortisol too. They also found that those children were more likely to have higher levels of perceived anxiety (*we're getting to that later*) as they got older too, as well as being more at risk of behavioral disorders, cardiovascular disorders and diabetes in adulthood.

Let's not forget that parenthood itself can be hugely stressful, faced with many challenges and difficulties from sleepless nights to toddler tantrums and teenage rebellion. It can be really tough going, so it's important to ask for help when you need it and be sure to use some of the methods we've already covered in this book to help reduce those feelings of stress and anxiety.

In fact, parenthood is one of life's greatest challenges. It's not like the should you, shouldn't you buy that expensive dress you saw debate. The dress you can take back if you change your mind, the kids you're stuck with so we need to help hold on to your sanity as much as possible.

PTSD

PTSD (post-traumatic stress disorder) is a mental disorder that can occur after a traumatic event has been experienced. Unlike acute stress, which occurs within 4-weeks, PTSD symptoms do not usually occur until four weeks after the event.

Causes of PTSD can include physical or sexual assault, war, natural disaster or acts of terrorism, or the death of a loved one, to name a few, and as women we are twice as likely to get this than our male counterparts.

There are certain criteria that must be met to determine if you are suffering from PTSD, such as the effect of the trauma on you and specific PTSD symptoms lasting more than a month.

In many cases after a trauma, symptoms may appear immediately and only last 2-3 weeks, in which case this is referred to as ASD (acute stress disorder).

Although ASD can sometimes make individuals more susceptible to PTSD, this isn't always the case. However, if it does occur, our mental state and perception of the trauma will influence the severity and duration of the PTSD symptoms

When PTSD does develop, a number of biological changes occur. The HPA and SAM systems we discussed previously become dysregulated, cognitive function is impaired, our startle response is enhanced and, changes occur in the brain.

The HPA axis experiences feedback inhibition due to chronically elevated secretion of corticotropin-releasing hormone caused by the repeated re-experiencing of the traumatic event.

This also causes the pituitary gland to become dysregulated. It releases less corticotropin and therefore lower cortisol release, and instead, the glucocorticoid receptor activity becomes heightened which stops the negative feedback signaling that would shut down the stress response.

Scientists have also found that several bacterial colonies in the gut were scarce in those suffering with PTSD, which means our gut health is not only impacted, but can also play a role in our susceptibility. I'll be talking about gut health in part 3 of the book.

IMPORTANT! - *Although this book will help you when it comes to understanding and managing stress, it is not equipped to help you with PTSD. If you do have, or suspect you may have PTSD, you should always consult a medical practitioner for the proper care and treatment. I have just added this in to introduce you to what I'd say is the most severe form of stress.*

The Link Between Anger and Stress

Do you find yourself flying into bouts of rage suddenly? If you find yourself quickly losing your temper outside of the premenstrual syndrome zone, then your stress could be to blame.

Anger is not as basic as just screaming and shouting at someone. It's actually defined as feelings of hostility, displeasure or annoyance and it is believed that those under a lot of stress and more prone to become angrier faster and, be less able to control their anger than someone who isn't stressed (*yep, that was me!*)

If you find yourself angering easily, whether that's over criticism, lack of acknowledgement for a job well done, being slowed down by others or simply know that you're hot-headed, then it's definitely an area that should be worked on as you're likely to project your anger in a negative way.

Negative ways of projecting anger could be that yelling and screaming I already mentioned, simmering away internally or expressing it through violent acts. So, if you don't find a way to manage that anger, it's going to become toxic. Worry not though, as I've got a few tips and tricks coming up.

If you think back to when we spoke about anxiety, we mentioned state anxiety and trait anxiety. When it comes to anger the same applies, as anger can be personality based (trait) which is chronic, intense and long lasting, or it can be temporary and short lasting (state).

Depending on how we express our anger depends on the techniques we use to try and alleviate it.

If you tend to hold your anger in and suppress it (*you know, when you're sat there internally grumbling away and feeling your blood boil but you're trying not to unleash the bride of Satan*), techniques such as breathing exercises or relaxation methods can help.

If you tend to express your anger outwards, towards others either verbally or physically then behavioral techniques, such as practicing patience with others can help.

Okay, so how does all this relate to your hormones and weight management? Well anger, just like stress and anxiety can activate the HPA axis stress response system (*Hello elevated cortisol*).

ANGER MANAGEMENT TIP!

If you're a fan of heavy metal, then blasting out that angry sounding song you love when you're full of rage could actually help decrease your levels of irritability and hostility.

Now, besides the obvious risk to our heart, anger can also affect both your immune system and your gut health. This is caused by increased levels of cortisol which can delay wound healing, increase levels of IL-6 (a cytokine) which accelerates our aging and, increase inflammation in the body.

This is why we need to regain control over those anger outbursts and that's exactly what we are about to do in the next exercise.

You'll be learning how to pinpoint the root causes of your anger and the emotions and thoughts you have, look at the situation from another angle and then, strategize a plan for future use.

By learning to recognize the emotions and thoughts you experience, you'll be better able to spot them emerging in the future and acknowledge their presence before they blow out of hand.

ACTION TIME!

Let's start looking at how to tackle those anger outbursts but, before you do, just sit comfortably and take a few slow and deep breaths in through your nose and out through your mouth to try calm your mind before we begin.

Don't be alarmed if thinking about the questions starts to make you feel angry again. If that happens, stop and repeat the breathing exercise until you're feeling calm again. We are digging deep into ourselves, our emotions and our feelings. It can be uncomfortable but, in the long-term it will be hugely beneficial.

Thinking about the last time you felt angry, what caused this? What thoughts or emotions were taking place (i.e. guilt, annoyance, jealousy, impatience, discomfort). Make a note below of all the ones you can think of.

_____
_____
_____
_____
_____
_____
_____
_____

What do you normally do when you feel angry? How do you behave? What do you do? (i.e. shout, throw things, punch someone or something, slam doors)

What does your anger achieve? What is the desired outcome of your anger?

What does your anger stop you from achieving?

Have you ever had negative consequences occur from your anger (damaged something, been given a warning at work, lost a friendship)?

_____
_____
_____
_____
_____
_____
_____

Looking back at what caused your anger, list all the things about the situation that made you mad.

_____
_____
_____
_____
_____
_____
_____

Now, try to put yourself in the shoes of someone who would not get angry at this. Why does it not make them angry? What strategy may they have used to deal with it?

_____
_____
_____
_____
_____

_____
_____
_____

Consider the answers to the last two questions. What is the difference between them? Has the situation changed? Has the individual's viewpoint changed? How could you apply this to help you next time you are faced with a similar situation?

_____
_____
_____
_____
_____
_____
_____

How did you find that exercise? Did you discover anything that you hadn't realised before?

Next, we are going to look at your stress resilience and your ability to cope with stress where I'll be introducing more techniques for you to try.

Stress Resilience & Your Hormones

Have you ever noticed how some people just seem to bounce back from stressful situations quickly and easily, whereas others seem to be wrapped up in their worries and anxiety for prolonged periods of time?

It's all down to our levels of resilience which are as unique to each of us as is our DNA. However, unlike our DNA which is something we are born with and unable to change, resilience is most definitely a skill that can be learned. In fact, you've already started building up your resilience simply by completing the tasks I've presented to you so far (and, there are plenty more to come!)

In addition to this, our hormones can play a role in our levels of stress resilience as a number of chemicals, peptides and proteins all influence this (including cortisol, serotonin, DHEA and testosterone).

When our HPA-axis is activated it releases DHEA in addition to ACTH and cortisol. DHEA is a precursor to androgens (those male hormones) which influences levels of testosterone and estrogen.

Normally, DHEA and cortisol levels are well balanced, helping to keep our mood and emotions stable. It is believed that when our stress response system kicks in, DHEA levels become higher which helps us be more resilient to stress. On the flip side, if we are constantly stressed, abnormally high levels of DHEA can be neurotoxic so it's always a good idea to keep those levels in balance.

Now let me share another interesting fact with you …

Have you ever wondered why the older we get, we seem to get more anxious?

I was discussing this with a friend the other day and we were commenting how after having children we were much less daredevil than in the years before we had children. We put it down to our having the responsibilities of parenthood.

However, in addition to this responsibility of a tiny human being to care for and protect, levels of DHEA actually decline as we get older which can also make us feel more nervous, anxious or worried … isn't getting older fun (*and we haven't even thrown menopause into the mix yet!*).

Our genetics (aka our DNA) can also play a role in how resilient we are to stress (now, I did say we can't change our genes, but we can change our gene expression through healthier practices and lifestyle).

That's because our resilience to stress is influenced by a brain chemical called brain-derive neurotrophic factor (BDNF). As well as influencing our stress resilience, it plays a role in our memory and learning, so when we start to get that foggy head, forgetfulness and inability to concentrate, it could be because this isn't working as it should for us.

BDNF is produced by the BDNF gene (*yeah, yeah, original, I know!*) however, scientific research found that some people have a variant in this gene (known as the Val66Met variant) which appears to be more common in people who suffer with anxiety and depression.

It was also discovered that in those who carry the Val66Met variant were also more inclined to ruminate over past events (we will be will looking at rumination in part 2 of this book).

Your Ability to Cope

Our stress resilience is also linked with our ability to cope. This refers to the thoughts, emotions and actions we use to deal with a demanding (or stressful) situation and each one of us will have a different way of coping with stress.

There are two primary coping approaches; problem-focused coping, which relates to finding active ways to tackle the unwanted circumstances or stressors, and emotion-focused coping, which focusses on managing the feelings as opposed to the circumstances.

These coping approaches can be broken down further into a series of coping mechanisms. We often use a combination of coping mechanisms dependent on the challenges we face however, we all have a set of "core mechanisms" which are the ones we use more often and are effectively our "go-to" methods of coping with difficulties.

For some of us, we like to plan, strategize and approach it head on, for others it's all to overwhelming and we prefer to avoid the situation and bury our heads in the sand.

However, just as with avoidance, not all of our coping mechanisms serve us well and we may find we are prone to fall into harmful practices in a bid to cope with our thoughts and feelings, such as alcohol (*which I've already admitted was one of my main coping mechanisms*) or substance abuse.

The 15 main types of coping mechanisms are:

- **Positive reinterpretation and growth** – reframing the situation in a more positive manner and growing from the experience.

- **Mental disengagement** – turning to work or other activities to prevent thinking about the problem.

- **Venting of emotions** – emotional outbursts and the need to openly express your feelings and emotions.

- **Denial** – refusal to believe the problem is real.

- **Spiritual coping** – using faith or spirituality for comfort and support.

- **Use of an emotional social support** – seeking sympathy from friends, family or anyone else who will give it.

- **Acceptance** – learning to accept the problem.

- **Use of instrumental social support** – seeking out advice on what to do from others, this could be friends, family or specialists.

- **Active coping** – taking actionable steps to eliminate the problem.

- **Humor** – laughing and joking about the situation to make light of it.

- **Behavior disengagement** – giving up in your attempts to deal with the problem as you feel like you can't deal with it.

- **Restraint** – not acting out impulsively but instead, waiting for the right moment to act.

- **Substance use** – resorting to alcohol, drugs, smoking, or food to make yourself feel better and take your mind off the problem.

- **Suppression of competing activities** – where you cannot think of, or focus on, anything else but the problem at hand.

- **Planning** – thinking about the problem and creating a plan of action for addressing it

ACTION TIME!

It's time to identify your own commonly used coping mechanisms. Looking back at the fifteen coping mechanisms above, which three are the ones you most use?

Coping Method 1: _____
Coping Method 2: _____
Coping Method 3: _____

For each of the coping methods you identified above, ask yourself:

Which situations do I use this mechanism in?

Coping Method 1:
_____
_____
_____
_____

Coping Method 2:
_____
_____
_____
_____

Coping Method 3:
_____
_____
_____
_____

Do I gain benefit from it? Why do I, or don't I, gain benefit from it?

Coping Method 1:
_____
_____
_____

_____
_____
_____
_____

Coping Method 2:

_____
_____
_____
_____
_____
_____
_____

Coping Method 3:

_____
_____
_____
_____
_____
_____
_____

Is this coping mechanism helpful, harmful or neither?

Coping Method 1: _____
Coping Method 2: _____

Coping Method 3: _____

As I've already said, your coping mechanisms can be helpful or harmful and hopefully you now know which yours are and whether they are helping or harming you.

The most helpful coping mechanisms are the adaptive ones which include planning, problem-solving, positive reappraisal and seeking social support.

However, there's always a fine line between just enough and too much so, you need to find the right balance for you as when a mechanism is becoming less helpful or harmful (such as if excessive planning was increasing your anxiety) you move into a maladaptive practice.

A maladaptive practice is one which may soothe your worries in the short-term but actually cause complications long-term. This includes practices such as disengagement, denial, and substance use.

Being adaptable to different situations and using a combination of coping techniques (such as problem solving and not rushing into things) can help you to successfully tackle stressors when they arise.

And a quick tip for you, avoiding the situation may help short-term, but long term its likely to increase your number of perceived stressors in the long-term, creating a snowball effect of super stress in later years. No-one wants that!

The key here, is learning and understanding your core mechanisms. This will help you to identify the harmful ones that you typically adopt and encourage you to find new, more beneficial, ways of coping.

As part of my stress management coaching, I carry out a through coping evaluation to help with this along with helping you on a more personal level to regain control over stress. If you'd like to know more, schedule a free discovery call from the coaching page on my website.

https://emmalouisekirkham.com

Avoiding Avoidance

Did you notice in the last section that some of your coping mechanisms were avoidance mechanisms (such as humor, mental disengagement, denial)? If so, then this section is most definitely for you!

It's so easy to try and avoid something if it's causing you stress but in life, we are always going to be faced with events and situations that may trigger us so we need to learn how to overcome this.

Learning to understand your avoidance patterns when faced with a trigger (the event) will help you set up alternative coping mechanisms but first you have to get comfortable with those uncomfortable emotions.

For example, work deadlines that need to be addressed can often cause you to procrastinate and adopt the thought process of "I'll do it later" as part of your avoidance however, as that deadline starts approaching your anxiety actually increases further and causes a snowball effect that could have been avoided had you not avoided the task at hand.

Firstly, you need to explore into those underlying emotions, then you need to identify your avoidance pattern … what do you do instead of addressing the task at hand?

Here's how you are going to do this …

ACTION TIME!

Step 1: Refer back to the 15 coping mechanisms and pick out the three you think you use most often.

Coping Method 1: _____
Coping Method 2: _____
Coping Method 3: _____

Step 2: For each of these, ask yourself the following questions:

- Does this coping mechanism support your goals and wellbeing in the long term?

- Do you use this coping mechanism to avoid unwanted events, consequences, thoughts or feelings?

- Do you use this coping mechanism to experience reward or pleasure?

Make a note of your answers below for each of your coping mechanisms,

Coping Method 1:
_____
_____
_____
_____
_____

Coping Method 2:

Coping Method 3:

Step 3: For each coping mechanism you said yes to avoiding ask yourself the following questions:

- What are the events, consequences, thoughts or feelings you are trying to avoid?

- Why are you trying to avoid them?

- How do they make you feel?

- What do or don't you usually do in order to avoid these events or situations?

- Do you think avoiding these truly help you in the long term and why?

Coping Method 1:
_____
_____
_____
_____
_____
_____
_____

Coping Method 2:
_____
_____
_____
_____
_____
_____
_____

Coping Method 3:
_____
_____

_____
_____
_____
_____
_____
_____

There are so many things we can avoid, including social interaction, putting off doing mentally challenging tasks, physical activity and, we can even avoid rest and relaxation by working long hours.

Our reasons for the avoidance can be just as varied, from avoiding actions, people or places that trigger painful memories, to not wanting to feel embarrassed, anxious, or even noticed. We can avoid doing certain things for not wanting to feel judged, or in case we do it wrong or, in case someone gets mad at us.

It can be uncomfortable searching deep into our souls for the answers but we have to do this in order to learn and grow. Once we know what we are avoiding and why, we can then start to retain our minds to address these challenges differently in the future.

To do this, we need to identify our usual patterns of behavior and then plan our responses for when the situation next arises so that we can handle it differently.

To identify your current responses, I want you to think of a recent event or situation that you've found difficult or challenging and how you responded to it. Make a note of the following points:

- The event or activity you've been avoiding

- How you responded emotionally

- Your thoughts behind the emotion

- What you did to avoid the event

Make a note of your answers below:

_____
_____
_____
_____
_____
_____
_____
_____
_____
_____
_____
_____
_____
_____
_____

Now we are going to plan what you will do differently, not just as an action point but also your thought patterns. We are going to make this a more positive experience so that the next time it arises you have a whole new mindset and approach to it.

Now, let me give you an example to demonstrate this:

Jenny realized she'd made an error with some documents at work (the event), she worried her boss would fire her (emotional response), she felt like she was incompetent and useless just like she'd been told in the past (her thoughts), she then avoided her boss all day and called in sick the next day (her avoidance behavior).

When Jenny then put the new technique into practice her answers were as follows:

Next time I make a mistake at work (event), my new emotional response will be to acknowledge the worry but understand I am having some difficulties with this (emotions), my new thoughts will be 'perhaps I need some extra support with this task' (thoughts) and my new behavior will be to speak with my boss about additional training so this issue does not arise again (new behavior).

That's kind of a quick and simple summary at basic level, but hopefully it helps you get the idea!

So, get that pen ready to make a note of your new way of coping by completing the following statements:

Next time I ....

_____
_____
_____
_____
_____

My NEW emotional response will be ... (you can still acknowledge the negative emotions that arise but this time you will have an alternative and more positive mindset)

_____
_____
_____
_____

_____
_____
_____

My NEW thoughts will be ...

_____
_____
_____
_____
_____
_____
_____

My NEW and alternative behavior will be to ...

_____
_____
_____
_____
_____
_____
_____

Oh, and don't just write it out. Remember to put it into practice too!

Part 2:
The Power of Mindset

What's your Mindset?

When we talk about stress and mental health we are referring to the health of our mind and our brain. However, it's often viewed in a negative way so, for this part of the book, we are going to be looking at mental health in a more positive light by focusing on changing our mindset.

But first, we need to understand what mindset we have, as this can influence on not only our resilience to stress but also our skills and our performance.

Our mindset typically refers to our assumptions, our ideas and our own methodologies. These 'mindsets' then influence our thoughts, emotions and actions - we will be looking at these differing areas throughout this part of the book.

Some of us will have a fixed mindset, typically those who are stuck in their ways. Some of us will have a growth mindset where we constantly strive to grow, learn and develop, and others will have a mixed mindset which means we adapt depending on the situation or circumstances that surround us.

In addition to this, our mindsets can be broken into three categories; personality, ability and stress.

Personality Mindset

A personality mindset refers to your personal qualities, beliefs and ability to adapt and grow as a person.

A growth personality mindset allows you to change and improve your personal qualities, whereas a fixed mindset restricts your beliefs and slows your personal development.

If you can adopt a growth personality mindset you can become more compassionate and dependable as well as being better equipped to improve yourself as a person.

Ability Mindset

An ability mindset refers to your views when you are faced with something physical or mentally challenging (such as learning or athletics).

A growth ability mindset drives you towards learning and challenging yourself mentally, which can improve performance in the long-term. A growth ability mindset can improve your attention, decision making skills, memory, motivation levels, perception and reasoning.

On the other hand, a fixed ability mindset is more likely to leave you disappointed and frustrated at the 'stupidity' of others.

Stress Mindset

A stress mindset refers to your beliefs around stress, whether you view it as positive or negative and, whether you shut down in the face of stress or rise to the challenge.

A fixed stress mindset could see you shutting down or becoming overwhelmed and panicked in the face of stress as you view all stress as negative.

Whereas a growth stress mindset believes stress is a positive thing we can learn from, which will improve your flexibility and understanding and, increase positive emotions.

If you are a person with a 'fixed' mindset, you'll find it harder to make changes as you are more reluctant to do so (*I'm a typical Taurean so I'm very set in my ways and dislike change at times*). This means you may give up more easily than others (*I'm definitely no quitter though*) and you will have a lower resilience to stress.

Interestingly, if you have a positive mindset when it comes to stress, it can benefit your hormones too. This is because those who have a positive mindset have been found to produce more DHEA (the steroid hormone that improves our stress resilience and our mood).

Worry not though, you're not doomed. Simply being aware of your current mindset and understanding where it comes from helps strip away resilience to change.

It is possible to move from a fixed mindset into a growth mindset. Previously, we looked at avoidance or acceptance as part of our coping skills, and mindset plays a similar role.

When faced with a task that seems difficult we can embrace it as a challenge and learn from the experience (growth mindset) or we can avoid it as it's too difficult and we do not want to be judged for our failure (fixed mindset).

The choice is always in your hands.

It's all about Perception

Now, at the start of the book, I mentioned that our stress response was dependent on our perception of the stressful event or situation.

Our perception is based on how overwhelming a situation is, how unpredictable our life feels or how uncontrollable a situation is.

When we review a potential threat, danger or stressful situation we use our own resources such as our past experiences, thoughts, beliefs and emotions to decide on how we will respond (or cope). This influences our actions and behaviors when faced with said challenging situation.

If we are a growth mindset, we are likely to rise to the challenge. If we are a fixed mindset we may find it more of a challenge to deal with which will lead to our having a more negative perception of stress.

Over time, this negative perception can develop into negative thoughts about ourselves, the world, and the future, which leads me to discussing with you another vicious cycle that can occur. If you've read my previous book, PMS Hell to PMS Harmony, you'll know I love to talk about those vicious cycles!

This particular vicious cycle is Becks Cognitive Triad, developed in 1976, which relates to negative thoughts, beliefs and perceptions about ourselves, the world and the future.

It's often used as a cognitive theory for treating depression but I'm mentioning it here to show the snowball effect of negative thoughts and beliefs that can keep you trapped.

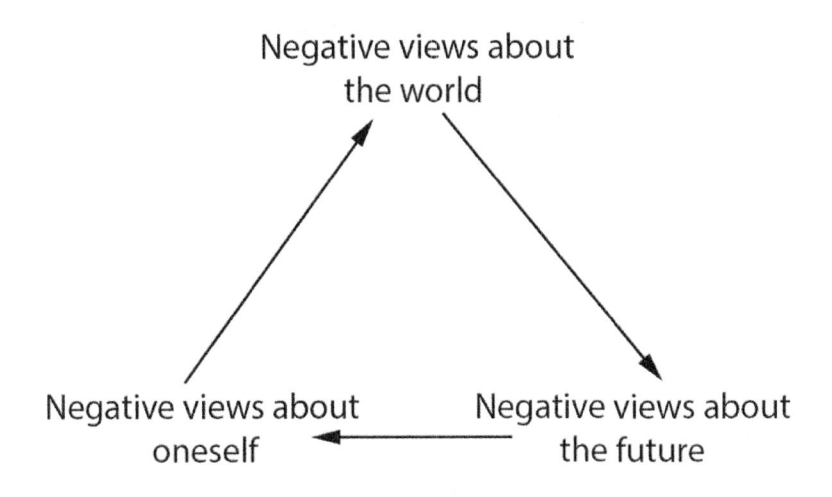

```
         Negative views about
              the world
               ▲
              ╱ ╲
             ╱   ╲
            ╱     ╲
           ╱       ╲
          ╱         ↘
Negative views about      Negative views about
      oneself    ◀─────────    the future
```

Figure 1 - Beck's Cognitive Triad

In simpler terms, this means that how you view a situation will influence whether the situation causes you stress or not.

If you have a neutral response to it then the situation is just a stimulus but, if you find the situation overwhelming or too much to handle, it becomes a stressor and those negative thoughts, feelings, and beliefs occur.

But, how do we decide if a situation is a stressor or not? First, our brain needs to decide if the situation is deemed as a stressor or not. The brain says "Yes, this is possibly a stressor" which then makes us consider our responses based on our own life experiences and views.

This is known as the appraisal system, during which we will decide upon the action to take; fight or flight, or even poor dietary/lifestyle choices as a coping mechanism.

The body will then adapt itself to the situation through these choices which can either be positive or negative. If negative this can lead to overwhelm (or in technical terms 'allostatic overload') which will have an impact on our endocrine system, nervous system and immune system.

But, can our perception mislead us?

It can if your emotions take over! And let's be honest, our emotions can change drastically from day to day (especially as women). However, even the scientists and researchers can't agree on a specific response to how our emotions play a role.

Three different models have been developed to describe the link between emotions and stress, and each theory has a different viewpoint.

One theory, the basic emotion theory, believes that an event can trigger a specific emotion. The constructivist theory, believes that a physical reaction to an event will lead to an emotional response, and finally the appraisal theory, which believes the emotion eventually arises after we have analyzed and assessed a stressor and our ability to cope with it.

Although there is some overlap between theories, the one thing that all seem to agree on in that an emotional response is present. What is most important when it comes to stress, is our perception (or viewpoint) regarding the stress and our perceived ability to cope with it.

Our coping mechanisms (which can be positive or negative as we previously discussed) are our ability to deal with a problem (through problem solving) and lead to the resulting emotions that occur (such as fear, anger or shame). The more positive the emotional response, the more likely we are to be able to cope better.

We will be looking at emotions in the next section.

Emotions and Feelings

Your emotions and feelings are often believed to be the same thing but actually, they are not.

Emotions are the physical responses that we display when we are triggered by situations, such as happiness or sadness. When emotions are displayed, we experience physiological, chemical and neurological changes in our bodies.

Feelings are the mental processes and reactions that we often hide from others. You know, like when the fella does something stupid and you just want to throw the book you're reading at his head but don't ... oh wait, maybe that was just the PMS!

How about that gut feeling? That niggle that you get in the bottom of your stomach that makes you feel uneasy and has those alarm bells going off in your head.

Those are the little warning signs linked to stress and anxiety that help to keep us safe. It's our internal alarm system that warns us that something is wrong, even though we often ignore it (*especially when it comes to dating the 'bad guy', been there, done that ... more than once!*).

However, stress can occur due to the intensity of our emotions and feelings which, as mentioned previously, is down to our thoughts, beliefs and perceptions.

Now, because our emotions can influence our behaviors and actions, it's important we understand why these responses occur if we are to regain control over them.

Our primary emotions are categorized as follows:

- Fear (includes anxiety, horror, shock, nervousness)
- Anger (includes annoyance, dislike, jealousy, resentment, frustration)
- Sadness (includes disappointment, grief, neglect, shame, pity)
- Joy (includes eagerness, excitement, hope, satisfaction, relief, pleasure)
- Disgust (includes boredom, revulsion, contempt)
- Surprise (includes awe, wonder, distraction, amazement)
- Trust (includes acceptance, hope, dependence, faith)
- Anticipation (includes having high hopes, interest, expectance)

We will generally experience a combination of emotions when faced with overwhelm to differing degrees of intensity.

Let's use gaining weight as an example. Your most intense emotion might be that you disappointed with the weight gain, or disgusted at yourself because of your weight (*I know, because I've been there*), but you may also be experiencing frustration as you thought you'd done everything right.

This battle of emotions in your head can fuel the stress within you, especially if you ruminate on it (more about rumination later). In addition to that, it can influence your behaviors and could cause you to give up in your efforts or resort to raiding the cupboards for comfort food.

If you can recognize and acknowledge the emotions, it can help prevent you from acting out those behaviors that won't serve you well.

However, if you can't recognize and describe your emotions, you may be suffering from emotional blindness. It's estimated that around 9% of the general population suffer from this (and its slightly more common in men than women, and in those with autism, Asperger's and PTSD).

Emotional blindness, also known as alexithymia, is used when you are confused about what emotions you are feeling and can't find the right words to describe them. You may also find it difficult to identify other people's emotions.

In this situation, you are more likely to struggle with stressful situations and, also adopt negative coping habits such as alcohol and drug use. As uncomfortable as it may be, getting in touch with your emotions can be hugely beneficial by helping improve your resilience to stress.

You can practice identifying the emotions of others by watching television with the sound off, watching the facial expressions of the people on the screen and guessing what they are feeling.

Alternatively, head on over to a local café, grab a coffee and do a spot of people watching. If you're brave enough, you could even strike up a conversation with someone to find out if your hunch on their emotions was correct!

To work on your own emotions, daily journaling can be hugely beneficial to help get thoughts from your head onto paper and let those emotions spill out onto paper. Reading back what you've written, you can then try to see which emotions from the list above are present.

Can You Regulate Your Emotions?

So, we've touched on our emotions and feelings and their influence on our experience of stress and, I gave you a couple of ways to get more in touch with your emotional radar both towards yourself and towards others.

But can we improve our experience around our emotions and feelings?

We can, through a process known as emotional regulation, which can be done either consciously or subconsciously. It is a three-step process that includes monitoring, evaluating and modifying. So, we would monitor our emotions or feelings, evaluate where these came from and if they served us well or not, and modify our actions and behaviors moving forwards.

We've already been doing some of this with some of our previous exercises, all of which help to build up our emotional intelligence.

Emotional intelligence is the ability to identify, harness and manage your emotions, and the emotions of others around you. It's the skill of being able to put yourself in someone else's shoes and being able to understand what they are thinking and why they are behaving as they do, which is a great thing to have if you work in customer service!

The higher your level of emotional intelligence the more able you are to face challenges and pressure, which also means your ability to handle stress is better too, and less stress is the aim here after all!

It's also believed that we may get more emotionally intelligent as we age due to learning from our life experiences and the fact we become more satisfied with our lives when older. Well, there had to be some perk to getting older, right, as opposed to it just being menopause and a Tena lady subscription to look forward to?

You can improve your level of emotional intelligence by learning to read the emotions of others (through the television example I mentioned previously) and, by becoming aware of your own emotions (through journaling, as I also mentioned).

Some questions to consider when working on your own emotions, and when journaling, to help improve your emotional intelligence include:

- Which emotions do I want to be more aware of in myself?

- Which emotions do I feel are the most disruptive to my life?

- Which emotions make me want to be the best version of myself?

Another way you can improve your emotional intelligence is to work on improving your listening skills when you are speaking to others. No one wants to be unheard but, we live in a world where everything is so instant, our attention spans have diminished and no one truly listens anymore.

It's definitely a skill I had to develop when I did my health coach training as I can be a real chatterbox. I really had to learn to shut my mouth to give clients the space and time to process their thoughts and speak them out loud.

Here's a few pointers for improving those active listening skills:

- Ask open ended questions that are relevant.
- Ask questions to clarify what has been said.
- Smile and nod to show you are listening.
- Mirror what someone has said by repeating this back to them.
- Keep eye contact (but not in a stare-you-out or creepy kind of way).

In addition to that, empathy goes a long way. Empathy is the ability to understand and share the feelings of others. Some of us have it in abundance so it just comes naturally to us, others struggle with it. If you are the latter and find you struggle with empathy, then don't worry, it is something that can be learned with practice.

Some great phrases to help you get started with empathy include:

- I can only imagine how you must have felt.
- I hear in your voice that that must have been difficult/exciting/worrying for you.

- If I was in your position I would have felt just the same as you do.

If you're a natural empath, this can bring its own set of problems … I've been known to cry along with a client as I've actually been able to feel their pain. I'm really sensitive to the emotions of others so, I can tell when someone close to me is troubled or worried, even when they try to hide it from me.

However, don't let that put you off! Empathy towards others is a great skill to have, plus it helps build stress resilience. So, next time you're having a conversation with someone give these skills a try to help enhance your emotional intelligence.

Your Thoughts Matter

We've discussed the link between our emotions, thoughts and actions a few times now so, it comes as no surprise that out thoughts can either help or hinder our levels of stress.

Negative thoughts can lead to a negative mood and more stress, whereas positive thoughts can improve your mood and reduce stress levels.

Where does your thought process sit? Are you a glass-half-full or glass-half-empty kind of girl?

When I work with clients in a coaching environment we do a positive thoughts assessment to find out exactly how positive (or not) their mindsets are. So, I'd say for the next few weeks pay close attention to your thoughts and on which end of the scale they sit.

Our thoughts are both conscious and unconscious processes, we can think about them or, we can simply daydream away where we become lost in our thoughts. In fact, we have thousands of thoughts that flash through our mind each day ... some of which we don't even realize occur.

Our thoughts are typical broken down into four categories:

- Factual Thoughts (based on fact, such as a task you must do that day)
- Fantasy Thoughts (I wonder if ...)
- Future Thoughts (What if ...)

- Judgement Thoughts (typically self-critical of yourself or others)

It's typically the 'what if' thoughts that are most likely to cause anxiety and the ones most likely to have negative connotations associated to them.

When our thoughts are negative they are referred to as automatic negative thoughts (ANTs), which can lead to anxiety and is a risk factor for the development of social anxiety disorder.

One negative thought is not likely to be an issue, but as with real-life ants, they never come in ones and before you know it, your mind is overrun with all these negative thoughts eating away at you which can lead to cognitive distortion (irrational or exaggerated thought patterns).

These cognitive distortions have no reasoning or logic behind them, the thoughts are not backed up by fact, simply errors in our reasoning.

In fact, I experienced this myself when I was suffering with stress and anxiety, and it's also a big sign to me that those 'head demons' are creeping back into my mind. I'll give you an example:

I'd be driving along to the supermarket or work and notice a car behind me. I'd make several turns along my drive and so would the car behind me. I'd start to get paranoid the car was following me which would ramp up my anxiety and make the paranoia even worse.

Now, from a rational state of mind, this was merely coincidence. Perhaps they were heading to the same area I was, so it's logical they would take the same route but, when you experience cognitive distortions that logic goes right out of the window.

That's just one example from my own personal experience, but let me introduce you to the 12 main cognitive distortions experienced by us humans.

Many of these are commonly experienced by us on a daily basis, and as long as they don't become persistent it's not a major issue (so no need to book yourself into the looney farm just yet!).

- **All-or-Nothing:** Everything is just so black and white, there's no room for any shades of grey. It's a bit of a perfectionist (fixed) mindset, if everything doesn't go exactly as you expected it to, then it's an absolute failure.

- **Over-Generalization:** One negative event reinforces the thought process that "bad things *ALWAYS* happen to me" or "I will *NEVER* be able to do …"

- **Mental Filter:** You focus on that one negative aspect or detail until everything, or the whole thing, is negative (*remember the cognitive triad?*)

- **Discounting the Positive:** Anything positive that happens is dismissed as "luck" or, is disregarded in importance and viewed like that one good thing doesn't count.

- **Jumping to Conclusions:** Interpreting things in a negative light without the facts to back it up. I actually once did this with my ex-husband … He was being sneaky and secretive, always on his computer. I was convinced he was cheating and we had a huge row over it, only to discover later he'd been planning a huge surprise to propose to me. Whoops!

- **Mind-Reading:** Oh, if only this was a real skill we could use however, in this instance, it's the assumption that someone is thinking negatively or badly of you.

- **Fortune-Telling:** This is where we tell ourselves an outcome will be negative based on our un-factual predictions. An example would be telling yourself, "this is never going to work so why bother?"

- **Magnification:** Making the problem far bigger than it is and minimizing the positive side of it.

- **Emotional Reasoning:** The assumption that your negative emotions reflect reality. You feel it, so it must be true!

- **"Should" Statements:** When you tell yourself you "should have done …" or that your life "should be" a certain way. Yep, I'm pretty sure we've ALL done that at some point.

- **Labelling:** Attaching negative labels to yourself. As women we do this a lot when it comes to our bodies and our weight (fat, ugly, disgusting), or even mentally labelling ourselves (stupid, worthless, etc.). FYI ladies, none of it is true … it's your negative perceptions of yourself!

- **Self-Blame:** Blaming ourselves for something that was out of our control. The best example I can think of for this is when a man has cheated. We blame ourselves, wonder what we did wrong, what could we have done to prevent it? When the reality of the matter is, he was a complete sh*thead and there was absolutely nothing you could have done. In fact, goodbye, good riddance, adios!

What you may have noticed about these cognitive distortions is that they are all negative thought patterns and these negative thought patterns can increase our predisposition to anxiety and maladaptive (destructive) coping patterns.

ACTION TIME!

We can't change our thought patterns if we don't know which thoughts are negative, after all they've become such close and trusted companions! We need to learn to identify them which is what this next task will help you do.

From the list of cognitive distortions above, which negative thought patterns are most prominent for you? If it helps, think back over the last week or month at which of these thoughts have arisen for you, and under what circumstances they arose. Make a list of them below.

_____
_____
_____
_____
_____
_____
_____
_____
_____
_____
_____
_____

The other issue with our thoughts, is that the more we think of something, we strengthen the neural connection for it (meaning it's the easiest path for the brain to take) so, if this is a negative thought, your brain will automatically want to revert to the negative way of thinking.

What we need to do instead, is shift from those negative thoughts to positive thoughts, as positive automatic thoughts (PATs) and optimism have been found to make you more resilient to stress.

One way to shift your thoughts from negative to positive is by identifying your trigger (i.e. the event or situation that arises) and your usual automatic thought, which is what you looked at previously. You will then develop yourself a new positive thought to override the negative one.

A great way to do this is to think of what OPPORTUNITY the situation provides so, if we use a job interview as an example:

"I didn't get the job (*the trigger*), I'm such a failure (*labelling*), I can't do anything right (*self-blaming*), I'll never get a job (*over-generalisation*)".

The new positive thought pattern for this scenario could be:

"I didn't get the job. I'm disappointed but this will allow me to learn from where I went wrong and improve for future interviews".

Another great method is to use Implementation Intentions, these are "if-then" plans where you will plan your future behaviors in response to a potential situation occurring.

An example of this would be, "IF I make a mistake at work, THEN I will speak with my supervisor about how I can prevent this happening again in the future" or even something as simple as "IF I start to get angry, THEN I will leave the room and take some deep breaths".

  Give it a try and create yourself some IF-THEN statements:

IF _____

THEN

_____

_____

IF _____

THEN

_____

_____

IF _____

THEN

_____

_____

Are you an Overthinker?

I mentioned 'what if' thoughts previously and sometimes these thoughts will play over and over in our mind, causing us to overthink and get anxious, which is the focus of this chapter.

Now, I don't know about you but, I am a terrible over-thinker ... I've had many a night where I've laid in bed going over and over something in my mind, tossing and turning as I've struggled to sleep (which is also hugely disruptive to those hormones).

When it comes to overthinking, this can be either negative and unhelpful or it can be beneficial dependent on the type. The two types of overthinking are rumination and reflection and, we will often experience both in varied amounts. The problem arises when rumination becomes dominant over reflection.

Rumination can become negative when it is persistent and is a practice we need to reduce. With rumination, it is difficult to change thought patterns, most of which are negative and repetitive. It can contribute heavily to our feelings of worry and anxiety, and can make us more prone to sadness and poor self-image.

When we experience rumination we often dwell on things that have happened, replaying the situation and rehashing the things we said or did, the causes and the effects. It can be hard to shut off the thoughts that keep coming back into our mind and ruminating for long periods of time has been linked to maladaptive practices such as alcohol or drug abuse and self-harm.

Ultimately, rumination will have you dwelling on past regrets and then feeling anxious about the future (what is still to come). On top of that, it's believed that when you team rumination with the addition of stressful life events (such as a bereavement) you are more likely to experience depression.

QUICK TIP!

Here's a quick trick next time you find yourself experiencing unwanted rumination ... try a distraction question and let you mind dwell on that instead.

Here are a few distraction questions you can try, they may sound a little strange but it's because they are designed to distract your current thought patterns so, the weirder the better!

Why do I enjoy reading the books I read?

What does chocolate taste like? (Describe it in as much detail as you can)

Why is it birds can fly but we can't?

Why not make your own list of weird and wonderful question cards that you can go to next time your mind is in a state of overthinking? I know that your stress response system will thank you for the distraction.

Reflection, on the other hand, is often much more helpful and beneficial and can help us with problem solving when faced with challenging situations. It helps us to adapt to situations and be more flexible and resilient to life's challenges.

When we reflect, we search within ourselves, analyzing why we do certain things, our thoughts and feelings behind it and effectively, soul-searching (which we've already been doing throughout this book).

We may meditate upon a topic in order to search for the answers. This is done in a positive way, with the ultimate goal of understanding and solving the problem at hand.

Reflection allows you to review past events and then create a plan to implement for if the situation arises in the future (just like with the if-then exercise you just looked at). As such, it has a far more positive effect on your mind and body.

Can we stop ourselves from Ruminating?

Absolutely! You can retrain yourself and your mind but, as with anything, it takes time and dedication. Nothing is ever an overnight fix, no matter what anyone tells you!

Our brain has the ability to adapt, reorganize itself and create new neural pathways through an ability called neuroplasticity. In simple terms, the more we do something the stronger the pathway becomes. The stronger the pathway, the more likely it is our brain will default to that pathway.

In the medical world, CBT (cognitive behavior therapy) is often used and this has actually been found to help reduce anxiety and increase neuroplasticity.

In this book, I'm arming you with a whole toolbox of tips and techniques to help retrain those neural pathways. One of those techniques that we are about to discuss is mindfulness.

Mindfulness is a form of meditation which is based on being aware of the present moment, which is something we often forget when we are wrapped up in rumination. It's been found to decrease those repetitive negative thought patterns and increase cognitive flexibility, which helps you step outside of your own mental bubble, so-to-speak.

When you practice mindful meditation, you pay attention to your thought patterns and reflect on if they are useful or not, which helps to shift you from rumination to reflection. This can help you to be more adaptable and open to new ideas which can help you to either resolve a problem or make peace with it.

ACTION TIME!

The following exercise is a series of questions looking at your last episode of rumination. The questions are designed to help you acknowledge the feelings that arose, reflect on them and adapt your thought process in future.

Be sure to do this when you're not likely to be disturbed as there are quite a few questions and you'll want to take your time to really think about them.

Describe the situation, trigger, behavior or event that last caused you to experience rumination and repetitive thoughts that you just couldn't clear from your head. What caused this to occur? What were you doing? Were you with others or alone? How long did the swirling thoughts in your head last for?

_____
_____
_____
_____

_____
_____
_____
_____
_____
_____

What thoughts or images were in your mind during this episode of rumination? To what extent do you believe these thoughts or images to be true or untrue?

_____
_____
_____
_____
_____
_____
_____
_____

What emotions did these thoughts stir up inside you (did you feel angry, worried, sad, fearful, etc.)? On a scale of 1-5 (where one is the least and 5 is the most), how intense were these emotions?

_____
_____
_____
_____
_____
_____

What were the consequences of these thoughts? What physical changes did you experience (such as trembling, grinding teeth, heart racing)? How did you act or respond? Was this different to how you normally respond or did you freeze and find yourself unable to?

_____
_____
_____
_____
_____
_____
_____
_____

When and how did the repetitive thoughts stop, if they have stopped? What caused it to stop? How did you feel afterwards? What have you learnt from this that may help you change your thought patterns in future?

_____
_____
_____
_____
_____
_____
_____
_____

What would you like to change in the future regarding these thought non-helpful patterns? What would be the short-term and long-terms benefits of making these changes? How will the changes impact on how you think, act, behave or communicate? How will it impact on your relationship with others?

_____
_____
_____
_____
_____
_____
_____
_____

What evidence do you have to support that the thoughts were true? How about evidence to support they were not true? Do you believe that if you were to let go of these thoughts you'd feel better?

_____
_____
_____
_____
_____
_____
_____
_____
_____

What alternative explanations are there for the situation, event or behavior that occurred? Would being aware of these alternatives help serve you better in the future?

Had the ruminating thoughts been true, what is the worst thing that could have happened? How about the best thing that could have happened? What is the most realistic view of this?

If you had a friend who was experiencing this, what would you say to them?

_____
_____
_____
_____
_____
_____
_____
_____

What advice would your friend give to you?

_____
_____
_____
_____
_____
_____
_____
_____

Next time a similar situation arises, how would you like to feel or behave instead? How would these new ways of thinking move you into a more positive mindset?

_____
_____
_____
_____

_____
_____
_____
_____
_____
_____

What can you do in the future to help yourself should a similar situation arise? How will these actions benefit you personally?

_____
_____
_____
_____
_____
_____
_____
_____

      This is a useful exercise to do each time you feel like those negative thoughts are taking over. It helps you reflect upon them and identify patterns and thought processes (such as all or nothing thinking) and then, be able to develop action plans to try and take a differing view in the future.

The Power of Positivity

As you've learned, just like our mindset, emotions and thoughts can be positive or negative.

The ideal is to have more positive emotions and thoughts than negative ones, as this means we are better able to cope with stress and have a more positive outlook. This will improve our sense of wellbeing and assist us in our quest to hormonal harmony and easier weight loss.

When we train our mind to be more positive, we are better able to avoid those cognitive traits, such as mind-reading and biases, and build a more accurate picture of a situation using the actual evidence before us. This helps us to think of more options for solving the problem than we would when experiencing negative emotions, which helps to lower our stress levels.

Positivity is believed to help our stress resilience massively so, always focusing on the positives as opposed to the negatives is key! In fact, research found those who focused on the negative had higher levels of cortisol (that most unwanted stress hormone) that those who adopted a positive approach.

ACTION TIME!

Let's practice a little bit of positive psychology …

I know that if I asked you to list all the things you didn't like about yourself you'd be saying there wasn't enough space to write it all!

It makes me think back to an advertisement I saw once on the television several years ago, I think it was for the cosmetics brand, Dove, where an interviewer asked women to say what their best feature was. The women struggled to think of anything positive to say, but when asked the same question about their friend they could answer in seconds, and reel off several things that they loved about their friend.

So, let's flip it around and learn to appreciate ourselves a little bit more. In the space below I want you to write down all the good things about yourself, there's probably far more than you realize!

If it helps, set a timer on your phone for 2 minutes and race against the clock to think of as many positive things about yourself as you can. Aim to fill all the lines ... I challenge you!

_____
_____
_____
_____
_____
_____
_____
_____
_____
_____
_____
_____
_____
_____
_____
_____

How did you find that exercise? Did you struggle, or did it come far easier than you expected it to?

We all have so many positive things about ourselves but, we've been conditioned for years by the media to believe we don't just so they can sell more glossy magazines or more products aimed to tackle our insecurities and hide our "flaws".

Women who have had children and ended up with stretch marks or caesarean scars may believe they are ugly and scarred but, hell woman, those are your tiger stripes, your war wounds. Wear them with pride as they are proof that you are truly amazing.

You created a whole new person, you grew it inside you, you gave birth to another tiny human (even though they may now factor in to the causes of your stress!).

Do you get my point here?

If you struggled with the exercise, that's okay too. Just keep practicing as the more you do it, the easier it will become and in time, hopefully you will realize that all these positive things you've written about yourself are true.

Now, changing your emotions and thoughts from negative to positive isn't going to happen overnight. It takes practice. Small steps every day will help lead to those big results. This is why gratitude can be a great starting point … by thinking of one thing each day you are grateful for, you start to integrate that positive thinking into your day. I've got a section on gratitude coming up so I won't go into it here.

It can also help to do things that you enjoy regularly to actually have some pleasure in your life.

As teens, we often wish away our youth because of all the things we can't do yet (because we are not old enough). We think that life will be more fun once we are a grown up because we can do everything we couldn't before.

Reality check! Once we start adulting (which is highly overrated), we often get so caught up in cooking, cleaning, errands, work and family that we forget to make time for ourselves and do the things that make US happy.

Start embracing your inner child and do more of what will bring you pleasure! Not sure where to start? Then use the space below to list three activities or hobbies that you truly enjoy but haven't done for such a long time and make some time to do at least one of these each and every week.

1. _____
2. _____
3. _____

Affirmations - Do They Really Work?

Another way we can try to reframe our thought patterns, and support the brain in forming new neural pathways, is through affirmations.

In psychology, the term self-affirmations are used and one method is to write or talk about your core personal values. Your core personal values are your internal standards that will help determine your needs, desires, beliefs and decisions.

Our personal values are often hidden within us, we rarely think about them consciously, but they do help us determine what is important in life to us. Being aware of them helps us to connect with our true identity yet, so many of us rarely reflect on these.

Remember back to when I talked about my days working in banking, and how I mentioned the pressure selling wasn't in line with my personal values. One of my values is honesty, and I didn't feel it honest to push a product on someone that was not needed.

Once we have identified our core values, we need to base our affirmations around these, as studies found that affirmations based on your top ranked personal values have a more beneficial effect on your stress response that less important personal values.

So, if you have tried positive affirmations before and dubbed them as nothing more than woo-woo nonsense as you did not see any benefit, chances are it's because these were not built around your own personal values. Our affirmations need to be built around our own values and situations in order to provide real value to us so I would highly recommend trying again with affirmations that are true to your values.

In the 1990's, psychologist Shalom Schwartz determined that, as humans, we have 58 specific values spread across 10 value types. The importance of each of these to us, varies from culture to culture and person to person and in the next exercise, you'll be identifying yours.

ACTION TIME!

It's time to discover your personal values. Below you will see the value types and specific values listed. As you read over these, circle, underline, or make a note of the ones that resonate with you the most. Aim for **at least 5** and be sure not to overthink it … go with your gut!

SELF DIRECTION
- Independence
- Freedom
- Curiosity
- Creativity
- Choosing own Goals
- Privacy
- Self-Respect

STIMULTATION
- Daring
- Variation in Life
- Excitement in Life

HEDONISM
- Enjoying Life
- Self-Indulgence
- Pleasure

ACHIEVEMENT

- Influential
- Successful
- Ambitious
- Capable
- Intelligent

POWER

- Social Power
- Wealth
- Authority
- Preserving your Public Image
- Social Recognition

SECURITY

- Sense of Belonging
- National Security
- Reciprocation of Favors
- Healthy
- Family Security
- Clean
- Social Order

TRADITION

- Moderate
- Humble
- Devout
- Respect for Tradition
- Accepting your Portion in Life
- Detachment

CONFORMITY

- Self-Discipline
- Politeness
- Obedient
- Honoring of Elders

BENEVOLENCE

- Honest
- Forgiving
- Loyal
- Responsible
- Helpful

- Mature Love
- True Friendship
- Meaning in Life
- A spiritual Life

UNIVERSALISM

- Broadminded
- Unity with Nature
- A World of Beauty
- A World at Peace
- Wisdom

- Social Justice
- Inner Harmony
- Protecting the Environment
- Equality

Did you have several in a particular value group or were these scattered across various groups? Remember, there is no right or wrong answer ... we are all unique which is what makes us so amazing!

Now you have identified your personal values, it's time to list them in order of priority and identify your top 5 values in the space provided below.

1. _____
2. _____
3. _____
4. _____
5. _____

So, you now know your top five values, but why are these so important to you?

For the next part of this exercise, I want you to think about the value you ranked number 1. Why did you choose this as your number one value? What stories or explanations are behind this value?

Spend a few minutes thinking about this and then write down your reasoning below as it will give you a deeper insight into yourself.

_____
_____
_____
_____
_____
_____
_____
_____
_____
_____
_____
_____
_____
_____

Did you know that studies have found that the use of self-affirmations can actually reduce the activation of our HPA stress response system?

It has also been found that positive value-based affirmations about future events can active the brain region involved with emotional regulation and reward. Affirmations can also improve our ability to problem-solve in stressful situations, and increase motivation.

Well who doesn't want to dampen down that stress response and be better able to cope with stress? That is why you're reading this book right? So, let's look at creating your own personalized affirmations ...

To help get you started, I'll give you an example. If one of your values was curiosity, one of your affirmations could be: *"I will embrace new foods and experiences with childlike curiosity"*.

Based on your top 5 values, can you create a positive affirmation for each one? Make a note of them below and repeat them to yourself daily as a mantra.

1. _____

2. _____

3. _____

4. _____

5. _____

Compassion

Compassion is the term given to the feelings of kindness and care toward those who are going through difficult times. Self-compassion is when we direct this kindness and care to ourselves. So, my question to you here is, how compassionate are you towards yourself?

I would suspect that, especially if you are reading this book because you are struggling with weight loss, you are probably not being as self-compassionate with yourself as you should be and instead pick fault with yourself and chastise yourself when you've eaten something you believe you shouldn't.

Am I right?

However, there are benefits to being self-compassionate. When we are self-compassionate we experience more positive emotions, lowered levels of anxiety and increased resilience to stress. We will feel happier, more optimistic, motivated and satisfied, which is the aim when tackling the stress in our lives.

When we are not self-compassionate we are more at risk of depression, anxiety, fear of failure, self-criticism, body shame and perfectionism. All of these will increase your stress and sabotage your weight loss efforts as you put more pressure on yourself and become engulfed by those negative thoughts and feelings.

It's also been found that being self-compassionate can reduce rumination, which means you're not going to keep dwelling on that slice of cake you may have eaten. You've accepted you had it, have forgiven yourself for it and you're already planning for what to do next time a similar cake-related instance arises, as opposed to repeatedly beating yourself up mentally for eating it.

If you're not particularly self-compassionate, you can train yourself to be. I've popped an exercise below for you to try that will help develop those new and more self-compassionate neural pathways!

I'd recommend doing this every day for 5-10 minutes, either writing about the same situation or a different one. Be honest with yourself when writing, this is for your eyes only.

ACTION TIME!

What makes you feel insecure, ashamed or not good enough? What is it that makes you feel this way? Write down your answers along with the thoughts and feelings that arise below:

_____
_____
_____
_____
_____
_____
_____
_____
_____
_____
_____
_____
_____
_____
_____

Now, think about what would you say to a friend you cared about who was in a similar situation? Coming from a place of kindness, understanding and compassion, and thinking to how you'd speak to a friend (because you are your own best friend) write a letter to yourself below regarding the situation you described above.

After writing this letter to yourself, from that place of love, understanding and compassion, how do you feel now when you think about the situation you first wrote about? Do you have the same thoughts and feelings or has something shifted within you?

Be sure to practice this every day for at least a week to build those self-compassion skills.

Hope and Optimism

We've all got that one friend who always has a smile on their face, who is always happy and positive no matter what life throws their way. I'm NOT that friend for the record, especially if you catch me in a morning when I've not had enough coffee!

Optimism is generally thought of as having hope about the future and believing that good things are to come, either from our own actions, the actions of others or, sheer luck.

Yet despite my saying I'm not that person, I do believe that things tend to happen for a reason and that it's because something better is destined for us.

However, when you have low levels of optimism, you are more at risk of anxiety and depression and, if you already suffer from these conditions, you are more likely to have a more pessimistic view.

Whereas the more optimistic you are, the better able you are to cope with stressful situations. You also have greater levels of psychological wellbeing, confidence, self-esteem and satisfaction in life.

In addition to this, optimistic people tend to have a healthier lifestyle; eating more fruits and vegetables, partaking in regular physical activity, smoking less and only drinking alcohol in moderation.

If you remember back to earlier in the book when we looked at coping mechanisms, people with stress and negative perceptions of situation were more likely to smoke more and drink more as part of their coping mechanisms.

Optimism has the ability to help us recover faster after facing a stressful situation as it speeds up our cortisol response time (i.e. it lowers cortisol levels faster).

It also makes us release less cortisol upon waking in the morning (when cortisol levels should be at their highest) and less of the pro-inflammatory cytokine (IL-6) which are known to further activate the HPA response that occurs when faced with constant stress.

Crazy how just having a more optimistic view on life can help with all this, right?

However, if you seem to be a pessimistic person then it could be down to your genetics. One study found two variants of the oxytocin receptor gene (OXTR) which could impact on whether we are naturally more optimistic or pessimistic.

You can improve your levels of optimism though. One study found that writing a letter to your future self where we visualize a bright and positive future can help with this, so let's give it a try.

ACTION TIME!!

Imagine yourself one year from now, in a better place than where you currently are. Any struggles you have been facing are gone ...

How does this new life look to you? What are you doing? Is anyone there with you? How are you feeling? Build a clear picture of the future you, make it bright and vivid, the sights, the sounds, the scents, then tap into the emotions, thoughts and feelings.

Now, write a letter from the future you to the current you explaining how you got to where you are now. What steps did you take to get there? What challenges did you overcome? What did you keep along the way? What did you let go of along the way? What did you realize on the journey? What did you learn from it all?

It's worth pointing out that just like hormones, optimism levels need to be in balance.

We've already discussed about when we don't have enough optimism, but what about when we are overly optimistic?

This can actually make us reckless or have irrational beliefs (*such as Disney and his happy ever after malarkey*) which can then cause us further distress or worry when something unexpected occurs (like a job loss or marriage breakdown that we weren't expecting).

Simply put, don't end up in La-La land and keep your feet on the ground at all times!

Hope on the other hand, although similar to optimism, can be a desire for something to happen and our belief in ourselves that we can achieve it.

When levels of hope are low you may not believe in yourself and your capability to achieve your goals (*which you can by the way, you're reading and implementing the advice in this book so you're already way ahead of the others!*)

However, when your levels of hope are high, you are more likely to plan how you can reach your goals, create actionable steps and, are more motivated at working towards reaching them (*my business coach, Jenny at Female Entrepreneur School, would love that nugget of info!*).

Give yourself a little "Hope Therapy" by setting yourself a challenging weekly goal that nudges you slightly out of your comfort zone and list the daily action steps you'll take to reach that goal. I'll also be looking at goals and time management in more detail in part 3 of this book.

I've popped a sample template to follow below:

My challenging weekly goal is ....

_____
_____
_____
_____

My Daily Action Steps and To Do's to Help Me Achieve this Goal are ...

_____
_____
_____
_____
_____
_____
_____
_____

This is a simplified version but, you can expand this further by planning out the steps and to do's on an hour by hour basis and allocating time to them. In fact, that's something I often do as part of my business routine. I even schedule in the dog walks!

You can make this as complex and detailed as you want as long as it works for you. Just remember, we all have the same 24 days hours in a day, it's simply how we choose to use them that matters but do NOT overburden yourself, as this will be counterproductive to your stress management.

Gratitude

Gratitude seems to be the latest trend in wellness and has been rising in popularity year on year. It goes hand-in-hand with hope, optimism and compassion and it's hugely beneficial for helping build up your resilience to stress and restoring the Zen and positivity in your life.

All too often, we drift through life on autopilot (eat, sleep, work, repeat) and we don't ever consider what we are grateful or thankful for. When you practice gratitude, you put an emphasis on expressing your appreciation, wonder or thanks for the people, places, things or situations that have made a positive impact on your life or day.

It can be as simple as being grateful for the comfortable pillows that allowed you to have a good night of quality sleep, to being grateful to your other half for not kicking you out of the house after your last pre-menstrual tantrum (*if PMS is a problem for you, do check out my book* **PMS Hell to PMS Harmony**) or simply being grateful for birdsong outside your window.

In fact, simply saying 'thank you' for those things, people and places can actually increase your sense of wellbeing, your levels of satisfaction with life and of course boost that resilience to stress but it's a practice so many of us forget (myself included).

When you actively practice gratitude you not only improve your stress resilience, you also improve your motivation and self-esteem. However, just as with everything else we've discussed, low levels of gratitude can increase your risk of anxiety, depression and burnout.

Gratitude is also classified as a moral emotion, as it activates the pre-frontal cortex, the same part of the brain that is activated when making moral decisions. This part of the brain also communicates with our amygdala, which means that when the pre-frontal cortex is activated it can reduce the release of the stress hormone norepinephrine and therefore, help to keep us feeling calmer when faced with a stressor.

Here are three simple ways you can try incorporate gratitude into your daily life:

1. **Get the Family Involved** During dinner, whilst sat around the table, ask everyone to share something they are grateful for that day and celebrate in one another's gratitude.

2. **List 3 Things** Before bed every night, list three things you are grateful for that day and three things you are looking forward to for the coming day.

3. **Thank You Cards** Keep thank you cards at home and write one each week to someone who you appreciate for that week. Explain in the note what they did and why you appreciated it (you'll make their day!)

***BONUS POINTS** if you do a gratitude visit with a letter of thanks to someone you never thanked who in the past has changed your life in some way. Read the letter aloud to them when face to face explain what they did and how it changed you. Warning!!- Don't be surprised if a few tears are shed during the visit!*

Part 3:
Diet and Lifestyle

Manage Your Time to Manage Your Stress

Wow, here we are in part three already! Hopefully, you've learnt a lot about stress and the impact it has on you and, you've been practicing the techniques we've been covering so far and seeing benefit from them.

In this part of the book we are looking more at diet and lifestyle, starting with time management because aren't we all so busy rushing around, trying to cram as much as we can into each and every day?

We juggle jobs, families, housework, hobbies, social activities and so much more into our days that we often believe we have so much to do and not enough time to do it in.

This has led to our experience of what has been dubbed 'time famine' which makes us feel unhappy, anxious, trapped, helpless, overworked or worried.

When it comes to stress and time there are two types of time stress.

- **Time Constraints:** internal or external deadlines that involve a task needing to be completed within a certain time. I had this when I was creating this book as it was released as a pre-order with a specific release date … the book HAD to be completed by a specific date.
- **Time Pressure:** relates to our feelings of not having enough time to complete the tasks we need to do. It

can also mean we don't have the time to think or make decisions.

Your perception of time can also play a role in this. Research found that when we are fearful or anxious our perception of time is altered causing us to over-estimate the amount of time passing. This implies our emotions also play a role in our perception of time.

Some examples would be the feeling of time stopping when you have your first kiss with that super-hot guy you've been dating, the saying *'time flies when you're having fun'*, or how time seems to stop when faced with sudden danger and you're frozen like a deer in the headlights.

This is because the amygdala and the hippocampus both play a role in our perception of time, and as we've already discussed, they also play a role in our emotional regulation and our stress response.

Are you noticing how all the things we've been discussing are so closely interlinked?

What we have to remember, just as I mentioned back in the chapter about hope and optimism, is that we all have the same 24 hours in a day. The difference between feeling overwhelmed or feeling on top of you sh*t is how you spend that time.

This is where time management comes into play, helping you to prioritise, plan, get stuff done and spend the hours we have wisely instead of squandering them on a Netflix binge or endlessly scrolling through social media (*I'm so guilty of both of these!*)

In this section, we will be looking at goal setting and time management in more detail and I'm going to help you with setting clear, measurable and actionable goals, as well as helping you identify ways that will prevent you from getting sidetracked, such as prioritizing and delegating.

So, back in the chapter about hope and optimism we looked at setting a challenging weekly goal, and the steps to be taken to achieve it to help improve our levels of hope. When it comes to goal setting though, they can be so much more than this.

Personally, I like to set myself yearly goals. I then break these down into more manageable monthly goals, all of which will help me achieve the annual ones. Then I break these down further into weekly goals.

Once I have my weekly goals, I'll plan out the daily steps and tasks I'll complete that will allow me to reach them. It sounds a lot but it helps to keep me focused on the bigger picture and gives me something to work towards.

However, when we set goals we need to make these SMART goals, which stands for specific, measurable (how will you know you've achieved it), achievable, relevant, and time-bound.

If we look at this from a weight loss perspective, let me give you three examples:

A) I want to lose weight

B) I want to lose 14lbs in the next two months

C) I want to lose 40lbs in a month

Of the three, which do you think best fits the SMART goal method?

If you chose option B you're correct, as this has a specific goal of losing weight, its measurable as we have the

14lb goal, its achievable as 14lb in two months is just under 2lbs a week, its relevant (providing the goal setter actually wants to lose weight) and it is time bound as the weight loss is to be achieved in two months.

Option A is incredibly vague, it cannot be measured and has no time limit. Option C is measurable and time-bound but, it's simply not realistic.

ACTION TIME!

Give it a try and set yourself a smart goal below:

_____
_____
_____
_____
_____
_____
_____

Okay, so you have your goal and the time frame in which you want to achieve it, but how are you going to get there?

First, you'll make a list of all the steps you need to take to help you achieve that goal (*if we stick to the weight loss goal as our example, you might list meal plan, meal prep, food shopping, clear out crap from cupboards*).

Have a moment to think about this and list them all below:

___

Then, you need to consider all the other tasks you have to do; this could be work commitments, housework, errands, dog walks, after-school activities that you need to take the kids to.

Take a moment to think of the jobs you regularly do on a weekly and daily basis and make a list of these below:

___

I recently did this task and I honestly felt exhausted just looking at all the things I was trying to squeeze into each and every week. It was honestly overwhelming, until I acted to reprioritize and restructure it into something more manageable.

If you're like me, and you're looking at your list and going into a panic at the realization of exactly how much you do and wondering how the heck you'll fit your goals into all of that, then take a few deep breaths and relax. That's what I'm about to help with!

We just need to determine the importance of each of those tasks and prioritize the most important ones. Oh, and for the record … your personal goal is a high priority so don't let it get forgotten amongst all the mundane tasks like laundry!

Looking back at the two lists you created, prioritize each of these, with number one being the most important or urgent task. The least important tasks could always be delegated to other household members if you have that option or outsourced (such as hiring a cleaner).

I have to admit, when I lived back in the UK, my cleaner was an absolute godsend and the best investment. I've probably already mentioned how much I hate cleaning, or if I haven't, then here is my confession … I would rather gouge my eyes out with a rusty spoon than do housework. I find it a complete waste of my time and don't get any satisfaction or mental reward from doing it.

Oops, I digressed … back to the task at hand!

So, you've numbered your tasks in order of priority which means your number one priority is the first thing you will address. Once that task is completed, cross it off your list and move onto the task that ranked number two, then task three and so on, so on.

I don't know about you, but for me I get a huge sense of satisfaction from making lists and crossing off tasks as I accomplish them!

Here's a few tips to help keep you on task when it comes to ticking those to-do's off your list:

Limit Procrastination

Did you realize that we are more likely to procrastinate when our goals are not aligned with who we are and what we need?

Others reasons for procrastination include not having broken our goal into manageable steps, having an unrealistic timeframe, we don't see value in the task (*that's me when it comes to cleaning*), we are unable to track the progress, or the goal simply isn't our goal.

The best way to limit procrastination is to have a clear plan in place. Plan out each day, scheduling in all the tasks you need to complete. You may want to break larger tasks down into smaller manageable chunks so that you feel less overwhelmed.

Manage Commitments

Don't be afraid to say 'no'. It's the most powerful word and can stop you from getting distracted from the task at hand.

All too often, we are made to feel guilty for saying no to someone or we believe we should have an excuse for why we are saying no. You do not need an excuse. If the request is not aligned with your goals and you do not want to do it, speak up. It's so empowering!

Relaxation Time

Schedule in time for you too, it cannot be all work and no play. Whether it's time to read with a cuppa, going for a walk outside in nature or, indulging in some well-earned pampering ... for your sanity and your mental wellbeing you need some you time.

Ditch the Perfectionism

We can often be so focussed on having everything 'perfect' that we never get anything done. Get rid of that perfectionist mindset as it creates unrealistic expectations (*take this from the single girl who has unrealistic expectations about relationships ... thanks for that one Disney!*) and instead focus on success, even if that success is ticking off a task on your list.

Stress and Exercise

We are always being told that for health we should be exercising regularly. It is true, as studies have found that regular exercise reduces our symptoms of stress and anxiety, from aerobic exercise to yoga, and from tai-chi to dancing.

That's because regular exercise can increase dopamine, serotonin and norepinephrine, which play a role in the regulation of our moods. When levels are higher, our mood is lifted which is why our sense of anxiety often eases after exercise.

However, when it comes to weight loss, your hormones and stress, the type of exercise you choose could have a huge impact on how successful your weight loss efforts are as can the time of day you choose to exercise. This is because certain types of exercise, and the time of day that you do it, can actually increase your levels of the stress hormone, cortisol.

So, if you're a lover of moderate to high intensity activity (such as lots of cardio and beasting it at the gym) then it could actually be doing you more harm than good.

These types of activities can activate the HPA axis due to increasing levels of adrenocorticotropic hormone (ACTH) and the levels of circulating cortisol after exercise in the short term.

This is more prevalent in unfit women, which means if you are already overweight, you are more likely to have elevated cortisol than a woman who is not overweight.

In these circumstances light to moderate exercise would be more beneficial in helping to decrease the levels of cortisol in our bodies.

Resistance training with short repetitions and longer breaks between sets can help, as can anaerobic exercise, as it has been found to increase levels of IGF-1 (a protein also called insulin-like growth factor).

IGF-1 levels tend to decrease as we age, reducing neurogenesis (the growth and development of our nervous tissues) and reducing neuroplasticity (the formation and reorganization of connections in the brain that we've previously talked about).

Lowered levels of IGF-1 have also been linked to stress and anxiety so it's important to boost them as much as possible.

In addition to this, regular activity can help reduce oxidative stress, reduce inflammation (another cause of unbalanced hormones and weight struggles) and increase brain size, especially in areas known to shrink in response to anxiety, such as the anterior cingulate cortex. In other words, it's not just good for the body, but it's good for the mind too.

However, I did mention that the time of day you exercise matters too.

The best time to exercise, when you are experiencing or trying to tackle stress, is in a morning when cortisol levels are at their highest. If you exercise late at night, those cortisol levels can disrupt your sleep.

The key when it comes to exercise or regular activity, is to find something that you enjoy as you are more likely to keep doing it. Experiment and try different activities to find what works for you and what you enjoy the most.

We are all individual in our likes and dislikes. I know running simply is not for me, I've always said you shouldn't run unless your being chased so I guess I'm doomed if the zombie apocalypse ever strikes (*I think that's rooted back to a previous trauma where I was running for a bus, boobs flying everywhere and just as I got there, all red-faced, sweaty and out of breath thanks to being overweight, it drove off with everyone watching from their seats*) however, I quite enjoy swimming, yoga and Pilates.

If you are feeling in need of some inspiration, here's a few ideas you could try:

Aerobic Activity

- Walking
- Running
- Cycling
- Swimming
- Dancing

- Tennis
- Marshall Arts (Karate, Tai Kwando)
- Skipping

Anaerobic (Strength) Training

- Lifting Weights
- Resistance Bands
- Push-Ups & Sit Ups

- Yoga
- Pilates

Pick one for the coming week and try it out. If you love it, keep doing it and if you don't pick another one! Just like anything, it's trial and error when it comes to finding what works for you.

Stress and Gut Health

What's the gut got to do with it? (*Anyone else have an urge to sing that Tina Turner style, or is that just me?*)

I've mentioned previously how digestion can be impacted when we encounter stress as that fight or flight mode shuts down the bodily systems it deems unessential.

Considering our digestive system is one of those 'unessential' functions in times of stress, it should come as no surprise that there is a link between the brain and the gut. This is known as the gut-brain axis (GBA) and it's in direct communication with the SAM and the HPA that we talked about earlier in the book.

Stress can also be linked to the population of bacteria in our gut, and an overactive HPA response can actually deplete our protective gut bacterial colonies.

In addition to this, our vagus nerve connects the medulla oblongata in our brain to our intestines. It's the longest nerve in our body and, alongside regulating our digestion, it works at its hardest when it helps to lower our heart rate during our "rest and digest" stage, which means it can also help us relax faster after stress.

However, if you are experiencing symptoms of anxiety, trauma or aggression you are likely to be less able to switch off your stress response due to lowered vagal activity which will have a negative impact on your digestive functions and your gut microbiome.

Our gut microbiome helps to regulate our mood, supports normal brain function, and increases our resilience to stress. In addition to this, it plays a role in neutralizing toxins, supporting our immune system, supplying essential nutrients, and reducing the 'harmful' bacteria.

It's made up of a group of beneficial non-pathogenic organisms that live in our gut, including bacteria, fungi, bacteriophages, viruses and protozoa (or in simpler terms our 'good' bacteria).

In fact, our bodies contain trillions of bacteria, fungi and viruses, with our gut alone containing over 35,000 types (primarily found in the intestines and colon).

Provided our balance of good and bad bacteria in the gut is balanced, no problems tend to occur but, when they become out of balance and there is too much bad bacteria in the gut, this can cause issues such as gastrointestinal problems or IBS. It can also influence the severity of your premenstrual syndrome and have an impact on your weight.

Dysbiosis is the term given when the gut bacteria are out of whack and this occurs when there is either an increase in bad bacteria, a decrease in the good bacteria or both.

Stress has the ability to disrupt our gut bacteria, which is obviously why we are talking about it here, due to the fact that the gut-brain axis (GBA) is directly linked to our hypothalamic-pituitary-adrenal (HPA) axis.

Changes in our microbiome can lead to depression and anxiety symptoms, and anxiety, which increases levels of noradrenaline and glucocorticoids in the body, decreases the levels of our good bacteria and increase levels of bad bacteria.

To help support our bodies with the good bacteria, we need to eat both probiotic and prebiotic foods. Probiotics are 'helpful' bacteria that help promote the growth of the good gut bacteria, prebiotics are foods or supplements that feed the good bacteria.

Certain types of these helpful bacteria, including the probiotic lactobacillus and Bifidobacterium, have been found to dampen down the HPA stress response, ease the symptoms of anxiety and depression, and lower cortisol levels. Who doesn't want that, right?

Probiotic Rich Foods

Natural probiotics, that help to repopulate the good gut bacteria, are found in fermented foods.

These include:

- Yogurt
- Cottage Cheese
- Miso
- Sauerkraut
- Sourdough Bread

Prebiotic-Rich Foods

Once you've populated those good gut bacteria, you want them keep them fed and strong (*think of it like watering a plant to keep it alive ... which I must admit, is not my finest skill*).

Some good sources of prebiotic-rich foods include:

- Banana
- Asparagus
- Garlic
- Onions
- Leeks
- Jerusalem Artichoke
- Chicory Root
- Soya Beans
- Barley
- Whole-wheat

Other ways to support your gut health include:

- **Reduce your exposure to inflammatory foods:** The most common food groups known to cause inflammation are wheat, dairy, corn, soy and refined sugar.

- **Reduce your exposure to inflammatory toxins:** These include alcohol and synthetic drugs including antibiotics, which actually destroy good gut bacteria as well as bad.

- **Drink bone broth:** This helps with rebuilding the good gut bacteria and supporting it.

- **Eat fiber-rich foods:** Foods that are full in fiber include whole wheat, chickpeas, beans and lentils, fruits and vegetables.

Stress, The Gut and Your Appetite

In addition to our levels of good and bad gut bacteria, stress and our gut health can play a role in our appetite regulation.

Our appetite is regulated by several hormones including Ghrelin, PYY, Leptin, Insulin and GLP-1. These will work by inducing signals in the neurons located in the brain which then causes changes in our behavior.

Ghrelin is known as our 'hunger hormone' as it stimulates our appetite. Ghrelin is produced in the stomach when we haven't eaten for a while and tells us we need to get food. So, next time the hunger pangs strike and your stomach growls loudly when you're in a quiet room, you know its just ghrelin doing its job.

However, ghrelin is also linked to the regulation of our HPA stress response, as people with high ghrelin levels also had high cortisol levels and therefore, higher levels of stress.

When levels of stress are high along with elevated ghrelin levels, our reward (hedonic) response is triggered. This makes us more inclined to crave alcohol or drugs, or to ease our emotions through food, which will lead to overeating, weight gain and further anxiety or depression.

After we have eaten, peptides are released to reduce appetite. Peptides are effectively a string of amino acids that are a precursor to a protein.

One of these appetite reducing peptides is peptide tyrosine tyrosine (PYY) and no, that's not a typing error, it actually does have the double tyrosine in its name. Another, is glucagon-like peptide-1 (GLP-1). Both of these peptides act like hormones, they are released from the intestines and our neurons (the messengers between our gut and brain), and both are linked to our HPA stress response.

But, why do some of us go the other way, and instead of emotional eating, go off food completely when feeling stressed or anxious?

One explanation could be down to PYY secretion in the gut. Some research found that when we are stressed, we secrete less PYY from the gut which prevents those hunger pangs and decreases our food intake whilst increasing our anxiety.

When it comes to GLP-1, studies found that injecting animals with this activated the HPA stress response whereas blocking it, reduced depressive-like symptoms. This mean we need to try keep those GLP-1 levels down, but how?

You can help regulate your appetite signals by continuing to work towards that healthy weight, minimizing your intake of sugary, high-fat and processed foods, eating meals slower and looking after that good gut bacteria. It's as simple as that!

Stress and Your Eating Habits

As we've discussed, when it comes to stress our emotions and feelings play a huge role so, it should be no surprise that our eating habits can be impacted, especially when we've already discussed gut health and appetite regulation.

Emotional eating is the term used for when we use food to comfort us and ease our mood or feelings. In some people this is displayed as eating when not hungry or for the sake of it (usually high-sugar junk foods), whereas other people may skip meals completely when feeling anxious or stressed.

The main emotions and feelings (see those two cropping up again!) that can trigger emotional eating are sadness, anger, joy, loneliness, boredom and shame. I know I've been guilty of eating when bored or, when I'm celebrating I like to go out for a lavish meal so, I've definitely got an emotional connection to food. How about you?

There are obvious links between emotional eating and being overweight considering that when we eat emotionally we tend to reach for the crap foods. We are also more likely to experience anxiety or depression, which is no doubt going to trigger that emotional eating further. Oh look, another vicious cycle!

But how does all this relate to stress?

Several studies have been carried out on our food choices when under stress and it was found that when given the option of a healthy snack versus an unhealthy snack, the stressed individuals would choose the unhealthy snack.

You're also more likely to indulge in those crap foods and sugary snacks when you're on a restrictive diet. So, that fad diet that seems like the next best thing can actually trigger you to go on a sugar-seeking binge and start the cycle of guilt, shame and emotional eating.

Instead of that bingeing, we need to work on increasing our happy hormones, and you CAN do this through diet!

One reason that our emotions are linked to our food choices is down to an imbalance of the neurotransmitter for serotonin (you know, that happy hormone I've already talked about a few times).

Serotonin is generated from the amino acid tryptophan. 90% of it is made in the gut and the rest is made in the brain however, tryptophan cannot be made by the body so, we have to obtain it from our food supply.

I've popped a list of some of the main foods that contain tryptophan below for you so, be sure to incorporate these into your daily diet.

- Fish
- Chicken
- Turkey
- Eggs
- Milk
- Cheese
- Tofu
- Beans
- Sesame seeds
- Chickpeas
- Spirulina
- Spinach
- Oats
- Rice
- Quinoa
- Potatoes
- Banana

Now, for this conversion from the amino acid into serotonin to work effectively, tryptophan needs to reach the brain. You can help it do this by eating a diet that is high in slow sugar-releasing carbs as this helps increase the concentration levels of tryptophan in the brain. Or, in simple terms, it means your brain can make even more serotonin if you don't eat foods that cause rapid spikes in your blood sugar levels.

The best foods to include for this are:

- Whole grains
- Oats
- Basmati Rice
- Brown Rice
- Quinoa
- Sweet Potato
- Banana

Also, being sure to include the B-vitamins, vitamin C, Zinc and the Omega-3 into your diet. These can support the process of boosting serotonin production (I'll be covering vitamins and minerals later with you).

Let's not forget Dopamine either, it's our feel-good hormone and helps us be more resilient to stress. However, when we undergo chronic stress and have that constant elevation of cortisol levels, dopamine levels can increase too in its efforts to dampen down the stress. When this happens, the dopamine response weakens causing us to have less dopamine receptors.

When we have lowered levels of dopamine receptors the body cannot utilize dopamine effectively. This causes us to crave more dopamine in order to feel "normal" and often presents itself in reward-seeking behaviors such as eating.

Dopamine is created from the amino acids: tyrosine and phenylalanine. We can help our body to create more of this by eating the foods listed below:

- Almonds
- Avocados
- Chicken
- Eggs
- Bananas
- Broccoli
- Brussel Sprouts
- Potatoes
- Dairy Products
- High-Protein Foods

Stress and Blood Sugar Balance

We've covered how our eating habits and food choices can be influenced by our emotions and looked at some foods that can help boost our happy hormones. We also know that gut health matters, as everything we eat and drink ends up in our gut and, that our gut is also directly linked to our stress response system.

Another way we can help to tackle our stress through our diet is through blood sugar regulation, which is what we will be looking at now.

Several studies have identified a link between our anxiety and our blood sugar levels (also known as blood glucose levels), so it's a key area to look at when looking to tackle our stress. So, let's begin by looking at how blood sugar levels in the body generally work.

When we eat food, the pancreas releases insulin so it can prepare the cells to absorb the sugar. When the levels of sugar go down, the pancreas then releases glucagon which tells the cells to stop taking in the sugar however, this process may not always work as it should.

Eating carbohydrates causes our blood sugar and insulin levels to rise. How fast and how high they rise depends on the food being eaten, some foods can cause a sudden rapid spike, others can have a slow release with smaller spikes.

After a blood sugar rise, especially from those processed and sugar enriched foods, levels are going to drop again. The severity of the drop will vary depending on how high the levels spiked in the first place.

When blood sugar levels drop, the adrenal gland secretes epinephrine which signals the liver to release more glucose. The pancreas will also release glucagon, which converts glycogen to glucose which combined can lead to even higher levels of circulating blood glucose.

It's also believed that glucagon increases the release of adrenocorticotropic hormone and our glucose levels, which will further ramp up the stress response system causing that vicious cycle of stress – emotional eating – blood sugar spikes and drops – weight gain – more stress - food cravings to get that 'high' back – further elevated blood sugar levels and so on, so on.

Blood sugar imbalances are also linked to elevated estrogen levels, premenstrual syndrome, PCOS and a whole host of other nasty hormonal issues, as well as type 2 diabetes and in time, the development of metabolic syndrome, which is guaranteed to impact on your weight loss efforts.

So, what's the solution to the blood sugar problems I just mentioned? We need to change our diet to ensure the foods we eat have a slow and steady release on our blood sugar levels. One method for doing this is to pay attention to the Glycemic index values of foods.

The Glycemic Index (GI) was designed to help identify how high and how fast foods spiked our blood sugar and insulin levels by. The foods are ranked from 0 to 100, with foods at 100 being the most like eating pure glucose and sending blood sugar levels through the roof, and foods at 0 having the least effect.

High GI foods are the foods that are ranked 70 or more, These are quickly digested and absorbed by the body, causing sharper highs and lows in blood sugar than the low GI foods.

Low GI foods (those with a ranking of 55 or below) are the foods that take longer to digest and do not cause your blood sugar and insulin to raise as rapidly (think of these as the slow-release carbohydrates you often hear mentioned).

This means eating lower GI foods can keep levels stable throughout the day and stop those mid-morning or mid-afternoon snack-attacks.

When it comes to low GI foods, you want most of your diet to include these. Some low GI foods include:

- Most fruits & non-starchy vegetables
- Lentils
- Beans
- Peas
- Minimally processed grains

- Oats
- Brown Rice
- Quinoa
- Low-fat dairy
- Nuts & seeds

Medium GI foods are those that are ranked from 56 to 69. These should be eaten in moderation and include:

- Wholemeal Bread
- Beets
- Couscous

- Banana
- Breakfast cereals (like Weetabix and special K)

High GI foods are the foods that are ranked 70 or more. When you check the list below, you'll see its mostly crappy junk and processed foods, and definitely the foods you should reduce your consumption of!

Some high GI foods include:

- White Bread
- White Rice
- Biscuits
- Bagels
- Croissants
- Cakes
- Sugary Cereals

A quick search of the internet and you'll find several sites and PDFs listing the GI rating of hundreds of foods.

Don't Fear the Fat

I've mentioned previously how we tend to reach for those high-fat comfort foods when we are stressed in a bid to ease our feelings of anxiety. However, high-fat foods (of the crap variety) are linked to having higher levels of anxiety so, in reality, we aren't helping ourselves in the long-term.

That being said, fat is not the enemy ... despite popular misconceptions.

In fact, when I was a slimming World member back in my late 20's, it was all about red and green days (before extra easy got introduced) and the biggest thing I remember is the way low-fat and fat-free products were pushed. Mullerlight made a fortune from us!

The thought of eating an avocado put many of us into a frenzy. We couldn't possibly do that, it will use up almost all of our days 'syns' (the points allocated for treats and extras) due to it being so high in fat. Yet many of these low-fat and fat-free foods contained more sugar than their full fat counterparts (and it's the sugar that's the real enemy).

When I went on to become a consultant, I continued spreading the same message to all my members. However, since training as a health coach and studying around nutrition and hormones, I've realized the errors of my ways.

Fat is not the enemy. In fact, we need the healthy fats for our bodies to produce hormones (along with cholesterol) and they can also help support our gut health and brain and, help our bodies absorb the fat-soluble vitamins (such as vitamins A, E, D and K).

So, as you can now see, some fats can be beneficial and helpful to our levels of stress and anxiety, as well as helping that weight loss. In fact, when it comes to weight loss, we've been led to believe by those clever marketing companies that fat is the enemy when in reality healthy fats can support our weight loss efforts.

So, let's take a look at those healthy fats and how they can help you.

When it comes to fat, all fats are made up of chains of fatty acids. We have three types of fatty acid chains; short chain, medium chain and long chain.

Short chain and medium chain fatty acids provide our short-term energy and are absorbed into the blood stream directly from our GI tract (the gut). Long chain fatty acids are typically stored for later use, they are harder for the body to burn which is why you don't want to be having too many of these.

We also have essential fatty acids; these are actually long chain fatty acids that are essential to the body. We are unable to create them ourselves so must obtain them from our food supply. They include Omega-3 and Omega-6.

The optimal ratio of Omega-6 to Omega-3 is 4:1 however, with todays westernized diet, it's more like 20:1 which is why the majority of studies focus on Omega-3 when looking at deficiencies.

In fact, studies found that 75% of people with mental health disorders (like depression and anxiety) are deficient in Omega-3.

Both types of Omega provide their own benefits; Omega-3 can help tackle inflammation, while Omega-6 (which can be found in evening primrose oil) can help reduce depression and irritability, which means they can help with stress busting too.

Not only that, these essential fats can also help balance all of our hormones, which can help achieve optimal ovulation and in turn, improve fertility which can be impacted by stress. They also help us maintain an ideal body composition (as in it helps maintain a healthy weight).

For the purposes of this book, I'm going to focus on Omega-3, as this is the one we don't tend to get enough of.

Omega-3 is available in three forms; alpha-linolenic acid (ALA), eicosatetraenoic acid (EPA) and docosahexaenoic acid (DHA). Out of those three, I can probably only pronounce one of those correctly so chances of you ever seeing me on social media talking about them in their long form are slim to none!

In addition to the benefits I've mentioned above, Omega-3 has been found to improve both neuroplasticity in the brain and the symptoms of depression. Plus, the more omega-3 in your bloodstream the more serotonin too, which means more of that happy hormone.

So, what do we need to eat to get these essential fatty acids into our diet?

ALA can be found in flax seed (also known as linseed), canola, soybean, walnuts, and leafy green vegetables.

EPA and DHA are generally found in fatty fish, such as salmon, and in fish-oil supplements. Curcumin, found in the spice turmeric, has also been found to boost the levels of enzymes involved in the synthesis of DHA ... so whip out those spices and get creative in the kitchen.

Stress Busting Vitamins, Minerals and Herbs

Our bodies require over 50 vitamins and minerals in order to work effectively, yet 9 out of 10 of us will have some form of vitamin or mineral deficiency, and that's before we factor stress into the equation.

That's because stress has an amazing ability to rob our bodies of these essential vitamins and minerals.

We've talked a lot in this book about the chemical reactions that take place in our bodies, through the HPA axis, in our brain and in our gut. Around one third of these chemical reactions rely on some of our vitamins and minerals which means, if we aren't getting the right amount, those chemical reactions can be hindered.

When we experience vitamin and mineral deficiency we are more likely to experience issues such as hormonal imbalances, premenstrual syndrome, weight struggles, joint or muscle pains, fatigue and even infertility.

In this section of the book, I'll be looking at some of the vitamins, minerals and herbs related to stress.

Vitamin A

Vitamin A helps to support your immune system, has antioxidant properties and helps to maintain healthy skin. Now, although this isn't depleted by stress, if you have too much of it, it can actually increase symptoms of depression and anxiety. So, to prevent any unwanted side effects, it's best to ensure you stay under the recommended daily allowance of 800mcg per day.

B-Vitamins

The B vitamins are a group of vitamins that all play a role in cell metabolism and let's be honest, who doesn't want extra metabolism? They have also been found to reduce the symptoms of depression and anxiety.

However, stress has the uncanny ability to deplete the body's supply of these vitamins. It's a catch 22, right? So, I generally recommend all women consider taking a B-Complex vitamin daily.

Let's take a look of some of the B-vitamins that can influence our level of stress and stress resilience below:

Vitamin B3 (Niacin)

Vitamin B3 is important for blood sugar balance and for the creation of serotonin (our happy hormone) and melatonin (our sleep hormone). It also helps reduce inflammation in the body and supports both digestion and brain health.

Food sources include:

- Whole-wheat
- Mushrooms
- Chicken
- Turkey
- Salmon
- Tuna
- Mackerel
- Asparagus

Vitamin B5 (Pantothenic Acid)

Vitamin B5 is essential for brain and nerve health, in addition to this, it controls metabolism and helps to make anti-stress hormones. Stress is known to deplete the body's supply of vitamin B5.

Food sources include:

- Mushrooms
- Lentils
- Avocados
- Whole Wheat
- Celery
- Eggs
- Strawberries

Vitamin B6 (Pyrodine)

Vitamin B6 is responsible for the production of our hormones, including serotonin, it's also essential for brain function and is a natural anti-depressant. However, stress can rapidly deplete the body of vitamin B6.

Food sources include:

- Wheat germ
- Eggs
- Beans
- Lentils
- Chicken
- Turkey
- Tuna
- Cruciferous Vegetables
- Onions

Vitamin B12 (Cobalamin)

Vitamin B12 is essential for the brain and nervous system. It is needed DNA and SAMe synthesis and, helps to carry oxygen in the blood. It also assists our body in its natural detoxification processes.

If you are suffering with depression you may have a deficiency of B12 and B9 (folate). So, supplementing these could help lift your mood. If you need to know more about the best supplements for you, check out my Dietary Supplement Plans on my website.

Food sources include:

- Oysters
- Sardines
- Eggs
- Fish
- Cheese
- Milk
- Poultry

If you are vegan, you are more susceptible to deficiency of this vitamin so it would be best to consider supplementing this. However, it can be found in fortified rice, fortified soya milk or yeast extract.

Vitamin B7 (Biotin)

Biotin works best when combined with other B-vitamins and, just as with the others, it plays a role in our cognitive performance and helps our body use essential fats.

Food sources include:

- Cooked eggs
- Almonds
- Liver
- Salmon

- Herring
- Oysters
- Sweetcorn
- Watermelon
- Milk
- Tomatoes

Vitamin B9 (Folate)

Folate is essential for brain development and nerve function, plus it is involved (along with vitamins B12 and B6) in methylation, a process that forms and balances neurotransmitters.

As I mentioned when we looked at vitamin B12, people with depression are often deficient in both folate and B12.

Food sources include:

- Green leafy vegetables
- Cruciferous vegetables
- Asparagus
- Sprouts
- Wheat germ
- Nuts
- Seeds
- Beans
- Chickpeas
- Lentils

Vitamin C (Ascorbic Acid)

Vitamin C is like a super vitamin, as it offers so many benefits to the body besides its most well-known role in boosting our immune system.

It has a major role in the conversion of essential fats (such as ALA) into vital brain fats (EPA and DHA), it supports brain function, blood flow to the brain and communication between the brain cells.

It's needed to help produce serotonin and can help reduce the effects of stress on the body, as well as helping our body detoxify.

Deficiency causes a reduction in your ability to cope with stress, as stress depletes the body's supply of vitamin C causing an increased risk for anxiety and depression.

Food sources include:

- Oranges
- Grapefruits
- Kiwi
- Berries
- Lemons
- Peaches
- Apricots
- Strawberries
- Tomatoes
- Red Bell Peppers
- Broccoli
- Cauliflower
- Potatoes
- Spinach

Vitamin D

Vitamin D, our sunshine vitamin, plays a role in our bone health and helps us to retain calcium as well as regulating our immune system. Low levels of vitamin D has been linked to depression, although there's not been any link to anxiety or stress.

Even though vitamin D can be created by our bodies from the sunshine (hence it's nickname of the sunshine vitamin) many of us are actually deficient in this vitamin as we don't get enough sun exposure.

What we often don't realize is the amount of sun exposure we are exposed to is dependent on the use of sunscreen, air pollution and cloud coverage.

Food sources include:

- Herring
- Mackerel
- Salmon
- Sardines
- Oysters
- Cottage Cheese
- Eggs

Zinc

Zinc is a mineral that plays a large role in our mental health as it can help with issues such as confusion, lack of direction, and depression. It's also needed for growth, immunity, energy production and hormone regulation.

Studies have found people who are deficient in zinc are more prone to issues such as anxiety.

Food sources include:

- Nuts (especially pecan, Brazil nuts and peanuts)
- Haddock
- Shrimp
- Oysters
- Egg Yolks
- Green Beans
- Oats

Magnesium

Along with zinc, this plays a role in our mental health and wellbeing. It can regulate neurotransmitter levels, support communication between our neurons and can help us sleep (which is most welcome when anxiety has your sleep patterns shot to hell).

Magnesium deficiency can activate the HPA stress response system, so it's a good idea to keep on top of those magnesium levels.

Food sources include:

- Seeds (especially sesame, sunflower and pumpkin seeds)
- Wheat Germ
- Nuts (especially cashew nuts, Brazil nuts and almonds)
- Most fruit & vegetables
- Brewer's Yeast
- Garlic
- Potato Skins
- Crab

Potassium

Another mineral that can be depleted by stress, potassium has several roles in the body including blood sugar control by regulating insulin release, metabolism, maintaining fluid balance in the body and supporting nerve and muscle health.

Potassium is found in many foods, so there is no need to consider supplementing this.

Food sources include:

- Watercress
- Mushrooms
- Cabbage
- Cauliflower
- Courgettes (Zucchini)
- Pumpkin
- Parsley

- Banana
- Cocount

Herbs and Botanicals

Herbs and botanicals are often used in natural medicine and many have been found to have calming effects on the mind and body. Below, I've listed five of the more well-known one's for you that can help when it comes to stress management.

If you are considering adding any of these into your daily life then you should always consult with someone who specializes in herbal medicine and only take them under their supervision as they can have some pretty nasty side effects.

St John's Wort

This can increase levels of serotonin as well as reducing inflammation and oxidative stress in the body. However, St John's Wort can interfere with some medication (including anti-depressants and birth control) so always check with your doctor before taking this.

Ashwagandha

For thousands of years, this herb has been used to relieve stress, as it's said to improve your mood and suppress levels of cortisol in the brain. It also has anti-inflammatory properties and can help women who are suffering with PMS or menopause symptoms. However, it can cause upset stomachs, diarrhea and vomiting in some people.

Valerian

This can dampen down the stress response system and help assist in a good night's sleep due to its sedative properties. Again, it's not for everyone as in some people, it can cause headaches, dizziness, upset stomachs and insomnia.

Chamomile

Well known for its calming effects, chamomile also has anti-inflammatory and anti-oxidant properties. It can help with sleep, digestion and improve healing but can also have the side effects of allergic reaction in those allergic to plants of the daisy family, drowsiness and vomiting.

Lemon Balm

From the mint family, this herb can dampen down the activation of the stress response system and reduce cortisol levels. It's also been said to aid in digestion and ease the symptoms of depression. However, if you're looking to lose weight be warned as this can increase your appetite as well as causing skin irritation, nausea, stomach upsets, wheezing and dizziness.

Your Handy Stress Busting Shopping List

I've added in this handy shopping list guide to give you a quick reference point for all the stress busting foods I've mentioned throughout this book. I'd recommend highlight the ones you like so you can build your shopping list and plan your meals around these foods.

Be sure to try and have some variety in the foods you eat (*say's the girl who is a creature of habit and often eats the same foods over and over!*) as this can help with weight loss, if that is one of your goals.

When you stick to the same foods all the time your body adapts, which is why you may sometimes hit that plateau. As they say, variety is the spice of life!

Cruciferous Vegetables

- Cabbage
- Brussel Sprouts
- Broccoli & Broccolini
- Cauliflower
- Kale
- Kohlrabi
- Collard Greens
- Pak Choi /Bok Choi
- Watercress
- Red Radishes
- Argula
- Rocket
- Rucola
- Mustard Greens
- Turnips
- Maca Root
- Wasabi
- Daikon
- Tatsoi
- Swede

Other Vegetables

- Sweet Potatoes
- Yam
- Butternut Squash
- Pumpkin
- Spinach
- Green Beans
- Asparagus
- Mushrooms
- Carrots
- Parsnips
- Bell Peppers (all colors)
- Courgette (Zucchini)
- Aubergine (Eggplant)
- Beetroot
- Capers
- Radicchio
- Bean Sprouts
- Alfalfa sprouts
- Cucumbers
- Endives
- Celery
- Celeriac
- Artichoke
- Okra
- Sweetcorn

Fruits

- Lemons
- Limes
- Avocados
- Tomatoes
- Kiwi
- Berries (all types)
- Cherries
- Strawberries
- Apples
- Pears
- Plums
- Apricots
- Peaches
- Red Grapes
- Pomegranate
- Grapefruit
- Oranges
- Nectarines
- Melons
- Mangoes
- Papayas
- Sharon Fruit
- Pineapple
- Figs

Animal Protein

- Salmon
- Herring
- Oysters
- Mackerel
- Turkey
- Chicken
- Milk
- Liver
- Cottage Cheese

Beans & Lentils

- Red Kidney Beans
- Baked beans
- Cannellini Beans
- Mung Beans
- Black-Eyed Beans
- Butter Beans
- Peas
- Chickpeas
- Lentils
- Split Peas
- Black Beans
- Soybeans

Sulphur-Rich Foods

- Eggs
- Garlic
- Onions
- Spring Onions
- Shallots
- Leeks
- Scallions
- Chives

Gluten-Free Grains

- Millet
- Quinoa
- Brown Rice
- Sorghum
- Sago
- Tapioca
- Cornmeal (Polenta)
- Corn Flour (Maize)
- Buckwheat
- Oats
- Amaranth
- Gram

Nuts & Seeds

Be sure to consume nuts and seeds in moderation as they are very high in calories.

- Flaxseeds (linseeds)
- Chia Seeds
- Poppy Seeds
- Mustard Seeds
- Almonds
- Hazelnuts
- Chestnuts
- Pine Nuts
- Pecans
- Walnuts
- Pistachios
- Sunflower Seeds
- Sesame Seeds
- Pumpkin Seeds
- Hemp Seeds

Herbs & Spices

Herbs can be fresh or dried. I personally opt for keeping a good supply of the dried variety as my plant-keeping skills are next to non-existent!

- Parsley
- Coriander
- Fennel
- Carob
- Dill
- Turmeric
- Dark Raw Chocolate
- Chilli Peppers
- Cayenne Pepper
- Ginger
- Cinnamon
- Cumin
- Alfalfa leaves
- Thyme
- Oregano
- Rosemary
- Basil
- Mint leaves

Fiber-Rich Foods

Fiber-rich foods help keep you feeling fuller for longer, plus they help bind waste products (including excess estrogen) so your body can remove it as waste. Try to include plenty of fiber in your daily diet (25g minimum) and be sure to increase your water intake accordingly to prevent constipation.

- Apple
- Banana
- Broccoli
- Carrots
- Green Beans
- Green Peas
- Beans

- Lentils
- All Bran
- Rolled Oats
- Quinoa
- Brown Rice
- Rye Bread

Lactose-Free Options

- Tofu
- Soya Milk
- Yogurt (no added sugars)
- Almond Milk

- Hazelnut Milk
- Rice Milk
- Oat Milk
- Coconut Milk
- Carob Bars

Teas & Infusions

Hydration is key to both your health and weight loss. So many of my clients have complained they don't like drinking water so, here's some helpful and stress busting alternatives.

- Lemon Water
- Cucumber Water
- Green tea
- Black tea
- Oolong tea
- St. John's Wort tea
- Gingko Biloba tea
- Ashwagandha tea
- Kava Kava tea
- Chamomile tea
- Valerian tea
- Lemon-balm tea
- Passion flower tea

Handy Stress Busting Meal Ideas

Maybe you're looking at that shopping list and scratching your head thinking about what to make that won't be bland or boring.

Now, let me warn you ... I may have Nigella Lawsons curves but I am most definitely NOT Nigella in the kitchen. I do tend to opt for quick and easy food fixes but, here's a few suggestions from my basic repertoire to help get you started:

Breakfasts

- Chopped seasonal fruits topped with Greek yogurt, ground flaxseeds and crumbled walnuts (add a drizzle of locally produced honey too if you want it a little sweeter).

- Baked Oats or Overnight Oats

- Porridge (*so simple, yet deceptively filling. Savory porridge is a winner for me instead of sweet porridge, especially my mushroom and thyme version*)

- Crushed avocado and boiled (or scrambled) egg on whole meal toast or rye bread

- Sweet potato hash (literally dice up a sweet potato and sauté in a pan or skillet with whatever other veg you've got to hand with some seasoning such as

Cajun or cumin and paprika - *this works well as a lunch too*)

Main Meals

- Salmon served with roasted Mediterranean vegetables and brown rice

- Black bean chilli with polenta/brown rice/sweet potato fries (*works well as loaded fries with a bit of grated cheese thrown on top*)

- Lentil Dahl

- Chicken, vegetable and potato traybake (t*hrow it all on a tray, season with salt, pepper, herbs and a drizzle of olive oil and throw it in the oven for 30-40 minutes*)

- Homemade vegetable soups (*throw all and any veg combos into a pan with water and a stock cube, when all the veg has softened blitz it up. I always add some potato in as I like a thicker soup*)

- Bolognese made with turkey mince

- Turmeric chicken (*marinade chicken with olive oil, turmeric, lemon juice, and garlic powder*) with rice and plenty of green veggies

Snack Ideas

- Berries and cottage cheese

- Apple and peanut butter (be sure to be mindful of the sugar content)

- Egg Muffins (*in a muffin tin add vegetables/tuna/salmon/cheese and whisked egg, cook in the oven until a skewer comes out clear of egg residue, it usually takes around 20-30 minutes - works well for a grab and go breakfast too!*)

- Hummus and vegetable sticks (or crudités if you want to be posh about it)

- Homemade popcorn (*plus, it's fun to hear it all popping in the pan too. Just don't forget to put the lid on the pan or it will explode all over your kitchen!*)

Like I said, I'm no Nigella but hopefully, you can see that this doesn't have to be difficult. Obviously, the more creative in the kitchen you are, you'll create way better combinations than I do.

In fact, be sure to tag any of your culinary creations on Instagram with the hashtag #stressedoutbook so that you can inspire me too!

Sleep Away the Stress

We mentioned right at the start that a side effect of stress can be that you may struggle to fall asleep, or you may find yourself waking up often through the night. This results in your body craving those crappy foods in a bid to provide the energy needed to get you through the day ahead.

Lack of sleep impacts on your hormone health and your weight, causing an increase in your appetite, disruption to blood sugar levels, insulin resistance, as well as increasing both cortisol levels and inflammation in the body. These issues have all been linked to health issues such as obesity, fertility struggles and heart disease.

In fact, when it comes to weight, multiple studies have found that the average weight difference between people who got 8 hours sleep and those who got less was 3lbs for every hour under the 8-hour benchmark. Hand me the sleeping pills … I'll see you in a couple of weeks when I'm back in my size 10-12's.

In order to sleep effectively, our bodies rely on a circadian rhythm, which refers to the physical, mental and biological changes that occur in our bodies over a 24-hour period. Those circadian rhythms are produced by our biological clocks, which refer to our internal timing devices and not just the fact we are getting older and need to hurry up and reproduce.

Light plays a major role in our circadian rhythm and is often influenced by sunrise and sunset. However, artificial light that is so predominant in our lives these days, such as those from telephones, televisions and streetlights, can disrupt this.

The biggest culprit being blue light, found on smartphones and computers, which operates on a wavelength of 450-470 nanometers. This has been found to suppress melatonin levels (our sleep hormone) by twice as long as green light.

Something else that can disrupt your circadian rhythm is your chronotype (*another scientific word for you*!) which refers to how you function best throughout the day. Are you a morning bird or a night owl?

A night owl who always has to get up early for work is actually working against their biological clock and circadian rhythm, which can have an impact on their eating behaviors, hormone release, blood pressure and sleep patterns. The same applies to those early risers who force themselves to stay up late.

You need to work with your own body and your own patterns, especially if you want to lose that weight and regain that delicate level of hormone balance as it's been found people who are not getting the right amount of sleep and not working with their natural rhythms are more likely to experience obesity and metabolic dysfunction.

ACTION TIME!

Over the next week, track the number of hours you sleep each night and how you feel each morning; did you feel groggy and sluggish, or did you feel alert and productive. You can easily do this if you have a smartwatch that monitors your sleep patterns. If you don't have a smartwatch then on a piece of paper, or in a notebook, make a note of the following:

- The time you went to bed

- The time you fell asleep at (if it wasn't straight away)

- The time you woke up

- How many times you woke through the night, for how long each time, and the reason for waking

- How well rested you felt in the morning (well rested, a little rested, not at all rested)

This will allow you to see if you are getting the recommended 7 – 8 hours of sleep each night or, if you are experiencing sleep debt (when you're not getting enough sleep).

You will also learn to identify what length of sleep serves you best as some people function amazingly well on just 6 hours sleep!

Once you have an idea on how the amount of sleep you are having is impacting you, you will know if you need to make any changes.

Here are my top tips for supporting your sleep. Choose 1-2 of these suggestions to implement over the next week, then the week after, add another in:

- **Stick to a Regular Bedtime**: Your body responds better to a routine, so even if you feel like you can't sleep still head to bed at that pre-determined time.

  Even just lying there resting can help your body to wind down, or listen to some soothing music or a guided meditation.

  I listen to a chakra guided meditation sometimes and it always helps me fall asleep, as focusing on picturing the meditation distracts my mind from all the racing thoughts.

- **Cut Back on the Caffeine**: If you need your coffee fix, stick to only drinking it in the mornings as having 400mg caffeine (your cup of coffee will contain between 80-200mg) 6 hours before bed has been found to delay your sleep by one hour.

  In addition to this, caffeine will also decrease the amount of melatonin (our sleep hormone) being released by the pineal gland and we need that to help us get a good night of shut eye.

- **Avoid the Alcohol too**: I used to believe that the wine helped me relax, fall asleep faster and give me a better night's sleep. However, this is not the case as alcohol actually interferes with REM sleep, delaying the first cycle which therefore disrupts our entire night. In fact, in the past, when I've hammered the wine a bit too much, I've had hugely disrupted sleep and felt shocking for it the next day!

- **Create a Bedtime Ritual:** You probably have a morning one without realizing; I know I do. I get up, go to the toilet, brush my teeth and go for coffee … in that exact order, every morning.

  So, getting yourself wound down for bed using a process like you do when you gear up on a morning is just as important. Some things you could try include in a bedtime routine are:

  o Meditating

  o Journaling (*keep it positive and include what you are grateful for that day as we have already discussed how a positive mindset can support you when stressed*)

  o Gentle stretching or Yoga

  o Diffusing some essential oils to create a lovely aroma in the bedroom (*lavender is a favorite of mine but it's not relaxing for everyone, it can actually overstimulate some people and disrupt your sleep further*)

  o Relaxing in an Epsom salts bath then getting snuggly in your pajamas (*this one's a winner in winter*)

- Reading in bed (a paperback book is best) with a cup of herbal tea, such as chamomile.

- **Make your bedroom an inviting space:** Clear out the clutter. Make sure your bed is made, the pillows are plush, sheets are luxurious. The room temperature should be around 16-18 degrees (depending how many blankets you use) to prevent you being too hot or too cold.

   Perhaps you want scented candles (keep them away from the curtains though!) to create a beautiful aroma, some potted plants to help oxygenate the room and some gentle, soft lighting for ambience.

   This room wants to be the place you really want to retreat to. Oh, and ban the electronics, especially the TV which men seem obsessed with getting in there. The best saying that I ever heard was: "The bedroom should be for sleeping and sex."

   Make it your boudoir, make it as extravagant or exotic as you like, or keep it simple, clean and crisp. Whatever works for you.

- **Have an electronics curfew:** As I've mentioned, those artificial lights and the lights emitted by television, mobile phones and computers are high on the blue light spectrum. This not only overstimulates our brains but just one night of blue light exposure can cause you to have slower metabolism and decreased energy the next day.

Stop using electronic devices around 1-2 hours before bed and put them on silent so they don't disturb you when you are trying to rest. There is nothing worse than the ping of a message at stupid o'clock in the middle of the night.

- **Stop eating 2 hours before bed:** Eating just before bed actually activates your digestive system which disturbs your sleep. In addition to this, it can cause blood sugar spikes followed by a blood sugar crash that can also disturb your sleep and have you searching for the midnight munchies.

- **Don't exercise at night:** As we mentioned previously, exercise can stimulate cortisol production so you need to be cautious of what exercise you do and when, especially when it comes to your sleep. With the exception of a little gentle stretching, I'd say it's best to exercise in a morning when your energy levels are naturally at their highest.

Breathing Techniques to Tackle Stress and Anxiety

When it comes to stress and anxiety, you just need to remember to stop, pause and, breathe ...

I wasn't sure if I should have put this chapter earlier in the book or at the end, so feel free to let me know your thoughts on that. But, if you thought it should have been earlier, let's not stress about it when we've been working so hard to combat that. Plus, it's better late than never!

When we are anxious, nervous, stressed or feeling scared our breathing rhythm and heart rate tends to change. This can then add to our feelings of anxiety and panic us so, getting our breathing back under control when we start to feel stress and anxiety creeping its way in can help alleviate one symptom at least.

Breath retaining is one technique that can quickly help bring balance back to our sympathetic and parasympathetic nervous systems, helping us to feel safer and calmer.

It can help to clear negative thoughts from our heads and, with regular practice, it can help to quickly calm you down when feeling anxious or afraid.

There are so many different breathing techniques out there but this is the one I tend to use the most.

How to practice Breath Retraining

- Sit or lay down in a comfortable position and close your eyes.

- Breath in through your nose, filling your belly like a balloon and hold your breath for three seconds. *You can place a hand on your stomach so that you can feel the expansion.*

- Exhale out slowly through your mouth.

- Repeat these three steps at least once more but more if required.

    It can help to count the breaths in and out so that your concentration is fully focused on your inhalation and exhalation. I usually use a count of 4 when inhaling and exhaling, but find what works best for you.

    As you become more proficient at this you may wish to practice it for a longer period of time (such as 5 minutes) as part of your daily routine for either starting your day or winding down for bed, as well as each time you feel the need to help calm your breath, your body and your mind.

A Final Word on Genetics

Throughout the book, I've made several references to how our genetics can play a role in our susceptibility to stress, and research has found that some of our genes can alter the function of the neurotransmitters that are involved in our mood regulation.

These alterations can include the over-activation of corticotropin, and the hampering our serotonin activity. In fact, there are at least 30 different genes that can impact on this.

Now we all know serotonin as our happy hormone, and its primary role is to act as a mood stabilizer. However, in order to work effectively it needs a transporter molecule (5-HTT) to send it to our neurons and, for it to act, it also requires serotonin receptors to be placed on each neuron.

When we do not have enough transporter molecules or when having issues with our serotonin receptors, we are more likely to experience anxiety and less able to benefit from serotonins soothing effects.

But what causes issues with our serotonin transporters and receptors?

One cause can be our serotonin transporter gene. Some of us will have a longer code in the gene and others may have a shorter code in the gene which can influence our anxiety levels.

Research found that most people with the shorter gene were more likely to experience increased anxiety and depression.

However, it's not all doom and gloom if you've got the shorter gene as our experiences of anxiety are also influenced by our early life experiences and our environment (*remember back to when we spoke about our thoughts and emotions being related to our past experiences, which feed into our perception of a stressor*).

But what if you've got the normal gene and you still experience anxiety? This could be down to epigenetic signals ... sorry ladies, but I love the science!

Epigenetic signals are signals sent within the body that can turn on or turn off genes. This is commonly done through a signaling process called methylation where hyper-methylation can switch the gene off and hypo-methylation can switch the gene on.

Another gene that can influence levels of anxiety is the glucocorticoid receptor gene (Nr3c1) which can influence cortisol levels.

In a study conducted on the nurturing of mother rats on their offspring (through licking and grooming), those who were nurtured often had lower corticosterone levels and therefore low anxiety, as opposed to the less nurtured baby rats who experience high corticosterone levels and high levels of anxiety.

How does this impact us as humans? Well, it means that pre-natal stress could increase emotional and behavioural problems in our children just as we discussed back in part 1 when we looked at pregnancy and parenthood.

Remember, you can't change your genes, but you can support your body in whether those genes are turned on or off by adopting a healthier lifestyle and mindset (just like flicking on and off a light switch) which is exactly what you've been doing throughout this book.

Keep at it and work through this book as often as you need to!

Well that's all ladies ... you've reached the end.

Thank you so much for choosing, and reading, my book. I really hope you've enjoyed the book and gained value from the hints, tips and techniques I've shared with you.

As an author, reviews make a huge difference in helping someone decide whether to purchase a book or not, so if you have enjoyed it please

Leave a Review

It takes just a few minutes to do and would mean the world to me.

Thank you once again.

Emma x

About the Author

Emma Louise Kirkham is an author and health coach who specializes in women's hormone health. She lives in the Algarve, Portugal with her German Shepherd, Lucky, after leaving behind her life in the UK back in 2021.

Her passion for writing began in her youth, when she would rush through her schoolwork so she could pull out the exercise book given to her by her English teacher and write stories. However, she currently writes non-fiction and has had articles previously published in Irelands Own and Peoples Friend, as well as having been quoted in Eat This, Not That!

Having trained with both the Institute of Integrative Nutrition and The Health Sciences Academy in many areas surrounding nutrition and coaching, as well as working in the body contouring industry as a therapist and educator since 2014, Emma has made it her mission to help women regain control over raging emotions and health issues associated to hormone imbalance.

Now, she's sharing with you the knowledge and experience she shares with her coaching clients in her Hormone Hell to Hormone Harmony Book Series.

Find out more about Emma and her services by visiting her website:

emmalouisekirkham.com

Or follow her on social media:

Facebook: www.facebook.com/hormonehelltohormoneharmony
Instagram: www.instagram.com/emmalouisekirkham

Other Books by the Author

PMS Hell to PMS Harmony was Emma's debut book and the first book in the Hormone Hell to Hormone Harmony Series.

Whether you find yourself bursting into tears over the slightest thing, turn into a snarling hell beast or find yourself spiraling into bouts of depression and lethargy ... this book is for you!

PMS Hell to PMS Harmony will take you on a journey of transformation and help you to regain control of those raging hormones that raise their ugly head every month.

In the book you'll learn about the impact different areas have on your experience of PMS, from vitamin deficiencies to blood sugar levels, and the natural and easy-to-implement strategies for tackling these areas of imbalance.

Here's what others have said:

"I cannot recommend this book highly enough. There are many 'omg I did not know that' moments in the book, and I think every woman should read this book"

"Easy to read, informative, a game changer for women with PMS"

"Easy to understand, easy to relate to and definitely a few laugh out loud moments"

"This book is full of golden nuggets and practical tips. Emma breaks down complex theories and makes them simple to understand & implement. "

"This book not only confirmed things for me that I had long suspected, but also taught me lots of new stuff and gave me some practical tips as to how to turn things around."

You May Also Be Interested In

28 Day Hormone Reboot Detox

We all need a jumpstart every now and then. So, whether you've hit a plateau, feel stuck in a rut or just feel sluggish and lethargic, then the 28 Day Hormone Reboot Detox is for you.

It's a flexible alternative to juice detoxes that puts you in full control of your detox program. Designed to help women kickstart their hormone healing and weight loss efforts by clearing out toxins from their bodies (you wouldn't build a house on shaky foundations, right?).

The program takes you step-by-step through a four-week detoxification protocol, compete with video lessons and downloadable workbooks, that won't leave you starving and reaching for the cookie jar.

After completing their program women have lost over 7lbs, felt more energized, experienced clearer looking skin and improved their sleep. Who wouldn't want those benefits?

To get started scan the QR Code Below:

Printed in Great Britain
by Amazon